Home Storage
Projects for
Every Room

Home Storage
Projects for
Every Room
David H. Jacobs, Jr.

TAB Books
Division of McGraw-Hill, Inc.
New York   San Francisco   Washington, D.C.   Auckland   Bogotá
Caracas   Lisbon   London   Madrid   Mexico City   Milan
Montreal   New Delhi   San Juan   Singapore
Sydney   Tokyo   Toronto

Product or brand names used in this book may be trade names or trademarks. Where we believe that there may be proprietary claims to such trade names or trademarks, the name has been used with an initial capital or it has been capitalized in the style used by the name claimant. Regardless of the capitalization used, all such names have been used in an editorial manner without any intent to convey endorsement of or other affiliation with the name claimant. Neither the author nor the publisher intends to express any judgment as to the validity or legal status of any such proprietary claims.

Disclaimer
The home-improvement designs and views expressed by the author are not necessarily approved by Makita USA, Inc. Makita USA, Inc. shall not be held liable in any way for any action arising from the contents of this book, including, but not limited to, damage or bodily injury caused, in whole or in part, by the recommendations or advice contained herein.

pbk   1 2 3 4 5 6 7 8 9   DOH/DOH   9 9 8 7 6 5 4

Library of Congress Cataloging-in-Publication Data
Jacobs, David H.
  Home storage : projects for every room / by David H. Jacobs, Jr.
    p.   cm.
  Includes bibliographical references.
  ISBN 0-07-032404-2
  1. Cabinetwork—Amateurs' manuals. 2. Shelving (Furniture)-
-Amateurs' manuals. 3. Storage in the home—Amateurs' manuals.
I. Title.
TT197.J35   1994
684.1'6—dc20   94-10826
                                                      CIP

Acquisitions editor: April Nolan
Editorial team: Joanne Slike, Executive Editor
         Lori Flaherty, Managing Editor
         Jeff Beneke, Editor
         Joann Woy, Indexer
Production team: Katherine G. Brown, Director
         Susan E. Hanford, Coding
         Rose McFarland, Desktop Operator
         Toya B. Warner, Computer Artist
         Cindi Bell, Proofreading
Design team: Jaclyn J. Boone, Designer
         Brian Allison, Associate Designer
Cover design: Cindy Staub, Littlestown, PA
Cover photograph:Chris Eden, Seattle, WA..   HT1
Cover copywriter: Michael Crowner   0324042

Acknowledgments

I received the assistance and encouragement of a number of special people in putting together, photographing, and writing this book. I appreciate and thank the following folks for all they have done.

Jack Hori, senior vice president, and Roy Thompson, product marketing manager, for Makita USA., Inc., provided a wealth of support in many different areas. I am deeply grateful for their interest and continue to marvel at the superior performance I receive from Makita power tools and equipment.

I want to thank Francis Hummel, director of marketing for The Stanley Works, for his numerous contributions to this project. I enjoy excellent results working with Stanley hand tools and have found all of their hardware, closet organizer, and other storage components highly efficient and easy to install.

David Martel is the marketing manager for Central Purchasing, Inc. (Harbor Freight Tools). I am grateful for his support in providing tools, equipment, and accessories that helped to make many of the featured projects easier to build and install.

Many thanks to Tom Tracy, advertising manager for Eagle Windows and Doors, for all of his efforts. The beauty of Eagle's top-quality wood windows and doors combined with energy-efficient insulated glass make these products excellent additions for utility and large storage rooms, attics, and all other home spaces.

Likewise, ventilating roof windows and skylights offer enormous improvements for many homes and their storage areas. For their support and assistance, I want to thank Thomas Marsh, vice president of marketing, and Daryl Hower, business manager, for Leslie-Locke, Inc.

Campbell Hausfeld pneumatic tools, nailers, and compressed-air systems made quick work of putting together many home-storage units. I appreciate all of the efforts provided by Hilarie Meyer, associate merchandising manager.

My sincere appreciation is also extended to the following people and the companies or organizations they represent: Maryann Olson, project coordinator/public relations for the American Plywood Association; Betty Talley, manager of marketing services, and Jeff Barnes of American Tool Companies, Inc.; Tina Alexiess, product manager for Autodesk Retail Products; Patricia McGirr, marketing manager for Alta Industries; Victor Lopez, technical services manager for Behr Process Corporation; Don Meucci, marketing director for the Cedar Shake and Shingle Bureau; Kim Garretson and Rich Sharp for DAP, Inc.; Jim Roadcap for The Eastwood Company; Matt Ragland, marketing manager for Empire Brush, Inc.; Jim Brewer, marketing manager for Freud; Mike Cunningham, director of corporate communications for General Cable Company (Romex); Peter Fetterer, director of public affairs for Kohler Company; Dave Shanahan, director of marketing for Keller Industries, Inc.; Mario Mattich, director of public relations for Leviton Manufacturing Company, Inc.; Peter Wallace, senior vice president for McGuire-Nicholas Company, Inc.; Ruth Tudor, product publicity manager for NuTone; Jim Schmiedeskamp and Phyllis Camesano for Owens-Corning Fiberglas Insulation; Mr. Dana Young, vice president of marketing for PanelLift Telpro, Inc.; Greg Hook, communications manager for PlumbShop; Bill Cork, public-relations manager for Plano Molding Company; Bob McCully, vice president of sales and marketing for Power Products Company (SIMKAR); Rob Guzikowski, marketing manager for Simpson Strong-Tie Connector Company, Inc.; Jim Richeson, president of Sta-Put Color Pegs; Dick Warden, general manager for Structron Corporation; Marty Sennett for DuPont Tyvek; Beth Wintermantel, marketing communications manager for Weiser Lock; Timm Locke, product and publicity manager for the Western Wood Products Association; Philip Martin, product marketing manager for Häfele America Company; Karin Martin, marketing services supervisor, and Jeff Bucar, marketing manager for Halo Lighting; Robert Suarez, sales manager for Quality Doors; Matthew Smith, marketing manager for U.S. Ceramic Tile Company; and Sue Gomez, marketing customer-service manager for Zircon Corporation.

Brian Lord, Bob Greer, Jim Yocum, John Gittings, Steve Hayes, and Josh Pearson deserve lots of credit and my heartfelt appreciation for their hands-on help, witty words of encouragement, and entertaining antics. Van and Kim Nordquist did another outstanding job of developing and printing hundreds of photographs. Finally, I am thankful for the patience and advice offered by Scott Wakeford and Al Davis from the City of Mercer Island, Washington, Building Department.

My family deserves recognition for all of their assistance. I thank my wife, Janna, for her support and the wide variety of large and small tasks she so eagerly and promptly accomplished. Thanks also go to our parents and children and growing family of sons-in-law, grandchildren, and close friends; Grandma Grace, Grandpa Wayne, Nicholas, Luke, Bethany, Ashleigh, Matthew, Adam, Brittany, Courtney, Kirsten, Shannon, Joey, Terri, Steve, Whitney, Tyler, Michele, Jake, Ryan Stearns, and Steve Emanuels.

Finally, I want to thank Kim Tabor, editor-in-chief, April Nolan, acquisitions editor, and the entire editorial staff of TAB Books for their encouragement and support.

CONTENTS

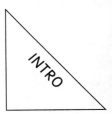

HOMEOWNERS STORE possessions all around their homes: clothes in closets; dishes in cupboards; food in pantries; keepsakes in bureaus; memorabilia on shelves; children's toys under beds; cars and much else in garages; seasonal goods in attics; and so on.

A young family moving into its first house after some years in apartments might be elated with what initially appears to be an abundance of closets and other storage space. As a well-seasoned family veteran with a wife and more than my share of offspring, I can state with absolute certainty that this elation will be short-lived!

People don't buy bigger homes because they physically grow wider and taller; they buy bigger houses to provide more room for their accumulation of clothes, toys, sporting gear, tools, household necessities, kitchen gadgets, memories, furniture, gifts, hand-me-downs, and other just-can't-be-thrown-away things.

Sooner or later, almost every homeowner has to hold a garage sale or otherwise unload a collection of good and usable objects. Let's face it, we homeowners can store only so much stuff. Fortunately, efficient home storage can help us to store our belongings more efficiently and conveniently, delaying or even eliminating the need to periodically part with our possessions.

Creating new home storage does not have to entail expensive, ornate, complicated, or elaborate components. Simple shelves, boxes, crates, baskets, and other plain containers placed in strategic positions can serve numerous storage functions. Short, plastic baskets filled with small toys can fit under beds; trays for spoons, forks, and knives can bring order to kitchen drawers; an extra closet shelf can keep off-season clothes out of the way; and small wood boxes placed on their sides make handy shelves in cramped sink vanities.

Most home-storage components utilize a form of shelf, box, or combination of the two. Build a wood box with a divider in the middle, mount it on a wall, and you have a cupboard. Set a board on top of two cement blocks to make a floor-level shelf. Put two more blocks and another board on top of that board and you'll have two shelves. Drive a few nails part way into wall studs to hang coats, hats, and a host of other items.

By putting more time and effort into such home-storage endeavors, you can turn otherwise ordinary boxes into attractive shelving units or cabinets. Instead of bricks, use vertical channels with brackets and smooth boards for shelving. Use a nice piece of 1-x-4 wood and some store-bought wooden pegs to build pleasant coat and hat racks.

Home Storage: Projects for Every Room is a basic building and installation guide designed for novice do-it-yourself homeowners. Although photos offer a variety of different home-storage options, the focus of this book is how such components are assembled and installed, with the goal of creating solid and efficient storage units.

Many home-oriented magazines provide readers with storage ideas but fail to demonstrate how these things are constructed, outfitted, or supported. Rather than simply supply more photos of finished shelves, cabinets, cupboards, and other units, this book concentrates on the work necessary to actually make them. Additional information explains how ordinary storage units can be made more attractive with the simple addition of trim or molding accents and the use of more exotic wood and other materials.

Along with instructions on how to design, make, and install basic shelves, cupboards, racks, and other useful storage things, photos and text provide novice do-it-yourselfers with advice on the safe and efficient use of an assortment of power tools and equipment, hand tools, and other home-improvement and woodworking implements. Once you learn how to operate these tools safely and effectively, you will feel able to tackle more intricate woodworking and home-improvement projects designed for custom applications.

This book is not intended to be an all-encompassing volume that covers every imaginable home-storage concept or design. Rather, it is geared toward helping you visualize how various types of home-storage units are initially designed, assembled, and supported so that you can build and install them yourself. Once these basic principles are understood, you should be able to determine how most any home-storage design is planned and assembled.

Before you begin any of the projects, commit the following two words to memory: Safety First! Always pay attention to the job at hand and the condition of your immediate working surroundings. Are family members standing next to your table saw? Move them away before turning the unit on. Are extension cords in your way? Piles of scrap wood in your path? Clear your work space and adjust power tool guards before you plug them in.

All workshops, garages, and other work spaces should have a fire extinguisher located close to an exit. In case of fire, you want to move in the direction of an exit to retrieve the extinguisher, not deeper into the burning room. Likewise, keep an all-purpose first-aid kit in your work area.

Projects that involve overhead work, like cutting away roof sheathing for skylights, require safety goggles. A hard hat is a good idea, too, generally costing less than $10 at home-improvement centers.

Operation of all power and striking tools requires the use of safety goggles or full-face shields. Likewise, plan to wear hearing protection while operating loud tools or machines like table saws, planers, joiners, and so on. Wear a dust mask while sanding and use an approved respirator while spraying stains or paints. Inexpensive dust masks are suitable for many dusty atmospheres. However, they are not designed to filter out chemicals commonly associated with paint or stain sprays.

Labels on paint and stain containers list recommended respirators. Units are available at most home-improvement centers, paint stores, and safety supply outlets. If you are confused about which type of respirator or filter cartridge to use, request help from knowledgeable store representatives. Keep extra safety equipment on hand so that your helpers can be protected, too.

Home storage ideas

"WHERE AM I going to put this?" Sound familiar? Homes are filled with huge assortments of all kinds of different things. Some are common, like eating utensils, cleaning supplies, and clothes. Others are special, like heirlooms, awards, and photographs. With that in mind, home storage can be categorized as either display storage or out-of-sight storage.

Shelves, hooks, racks, and open-front cases generally are reserved for those things we want to display proudly or have easy access to. Closets, cabinets, cupboards, and pantries store things that we need only occasionally or that we don't want everyone to see.

While contemplating your home's storage needs, be sure to account for convenience factors. Will you be retrieving certain objects on a daily basis or just once every few months? Frequently used items should be stored close to where they are commonly needed and used. Seasonal things and those saved for special occasions can be stored in out-of-the-way closets, cabinets, or attics.

Finding storage ideas

As an avid do-it-yourself homeowner, I have looked through many home-improvement and do-it-yourself publications over the span of many years, and I have picked up home-storage ideas and designs from sources too numerous to remember. Therefore, I cannot take credit for specific project designs, nor am I able to provide credit where it may be due.

My accumulation of home-storage ideas and the knowledge of how they are assembled and installed results from looking through magazines, browsing through model homes, inspecting friends' building accomplishments, talking with professional cabinetmakers, and practicing with tools and materials. This is how you can discover new home-storage trends and ideas, too.

Read an assortment of do-it-yourself magazines like *Workbench*, *The Family Handyman*, and others that are commonly available at libraries. Look through interior-design magazines. Newspaper advertisements for department stores, home-improvement centers, and specialty stores often feature pictures of storage systems that might be perfect for you. Go to home-improvement centers and study storage cabinets and other units on display. Inspect them closely to see how they are assembled and held together. Also investigate furniture stores, unfinished-furniture outlets, and other places that might carry items of interest.

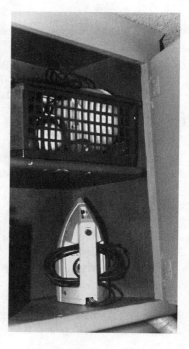

In a laundry or utility room, a simple plastic basket can hold light bulbs, extension cords, and a few other items. Containers like this can hold many small items and are easy to pull out of cupboards and look through. In a child's closet, they may be perfect for storing building blocks, play cars, doll clothes, and so on.

Living-area storage

Grandma Grace learned long ago that trunks are capable of holding lots of stuff. Some trunks have compartments that make it easy to separate the contents. Some people regard older trunks as antiques and use them as pieces of furniture. In addition to storing objects seldom needed, like family heirlooms and photo albums, this trunk doubles as an end table adorned with a lamp and plant.

An old ice box has been refinished to look new. Rather than function simply as a piece of furniture on display, this one holds video- and audiotapes and other television and sound-system components. Trunks, ice boxes, and other antique pieces can serve you well as both furniture accessories and storage units for living rooms, dens, family rooms, and bedrooms.

Cabinet and cupboard doors do a good job of keeping things out of sight. You may find some units are more convenient, however, if they don't have doors.

An open shelf unit made with A/C plywood and trimmed with fir molding holds an assortment of music sheets and books, and it can be located conveniently next to the piano. This unit was designed to be tall and narrow so that it could fit into a small space and remain out of the way of foot traffic. Shelf depth was determined by the width of the intended contents.

If you need to store lots of things in living rooms, family rooms, and other living areas, consider furniture pieces that also serve as storage units. Coffee tables, end tables, and entertainment-system cabinets can include both open and closed storage. A small, attractive wooden file cabinet can serve as both an end table and a storage center for important household papers.

Cupboards & cabinets

The dictionary defines cabinets and cupboards similarly, as pieces of furniture with shelves. For our purposes, let's regard cupboards as small cabinets normally located above waist level and cabinets as larger units placed at floor level rising to waist height.

Cupboards and cabinets are equipped with doors. Without doors, we would call them open shelves or cases, such as bookcases or display cases. Most folks rely on cupboards and cabinets to store things that they prefer to keep out of sight.

Home garages are notorious for becoming dumping grounds for everything from broken toys to Christmas boxes and old clothes to bicycle parts. Wouldn't it be nice to have a neat and tidy garage where your tools are handy and there is plenty of room for your car or cars?

A series of 4-foot-wide cupboards and cabinets provide this garage with plenty of enclosed storage and space for two cars, bicycles, garden tools, and working room. Each 4-foot section consists of A/C plywood bases, shelves, and side partitions; fir face trim (rails and stiles); and birch-plywood doors and end pieces. Birch plywood is used for these exposed pieces because it holds paint and stain much better than regular plywood. The main countertop is made from A/C plywood and then covered with a plastic laminate sheet, while the work counter in front has a top made from laminated 2×2s.

Typically, cupboards and cabinets are built in separate sections and then installed so that they appear to be a single unit. This is accomplished by allowing upright end trim pieces (stiles) to stick out past unit ends by about ¼ to ⅜ inch. The resulting gap between side panels allows room for maneuvering and squaring each unit. Trim pieces butt together for a completed appearance. You should be able to see similar gaps on the bottoms of your kitchen cupboards.

Shelves

Home-improvement centers carry a wide variety of shelving units. They are most often purchased in a box and require assembly at home. Prefabricated shelving units are available in particleboard, metal, plastic, and other materials. Styles vary, as do costs and accessory options.

It took the boys only about five minutes to put this Plano unit together. (See illustration on page 5). Tubes fit into holes located at the corners of each shelf. For convenience, tubes can be cut as needed to accommodate different shelf heights. To ensure maximum safety for units this tall, be sure to secure upper shelves to walls with screws or other fasteners. These shelves are equipped with holes along the rear lips through which screws are attached to walls.

Laundry rooms, utility rooms, large attics, garages, spaces under stairs, deep closets, sheds, and similar areas can be well served with open shelving units. In lieu of store-bought shelf systems, consider making your own.

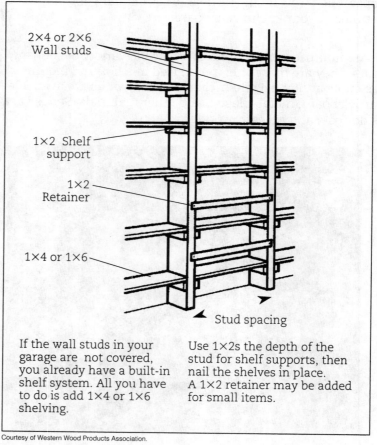

2×4 or 2×6 Wall studs

1×2 Shelf support

1×2 Retainer

1×4 or 1×6

Stud spacing

If the wall studs in your garage are not covered, you already have a built-in shelf system. All you have to do is add 1×4 or 1×6 shelving.

Use 1×2s the depth of the stud for shelf supports, then nail the shelves in place. A 1×2 retainer may be added for small items.

Courtesy of Western Wood Products Association.

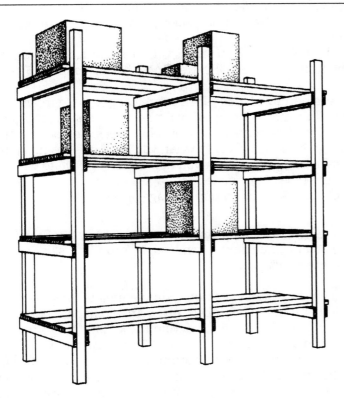

If you regularly transfer storables from room to room or garage to basement between seasons, a portable ladder shelf might be what you need. The shelf is easy to move and simple to build.

The unit's basic components are three double-rung 2x4 ladders. Cleats attached to the underside of the shelves fit snugly into the double rungs to lock the whole unit in place. To move the unit, simply lift off the shelves.

Make each ladder from a pair of six-foot 2x4s for the rails and eight 22-inch long 1x4s for the parallel rungs. Use a carpenter's square to make sure the foot of each rail is perfectly square.

Starting eight inches from the bottom of the rails, space the rungs 20 inches apart, measuring from the top of the rung. Fasten the rungs to the rails with 8d (eight penny) nails.

Each of the shelves is made from three parallel 10-foot 1x6-inch boards. Fasten the shelves together on the underside with three 2x4-inch, 17 1/2-inch-long wood cleats.   Place one cleat in the middle of

the shelf. Space the other two cleats one foot from each edge.

Measure carefully when attaching. the cleats because they must align perfectly with the rung openings.

You can vary the width of the shelves to suit your needs, such as two 1x12s for more width. However, make sure to adjust your other dimensions accordingly.

For added support, install 1x4 inch diagonal cross braces along the back (not shown in the illustration). Attach these to the back of the unit using bolts and wing nuts to allow easy removal.

Sand any rough edges or sharp corners. Paint the completed unit, or apply a clear finish to protect the wood.

Materials Needed: 6 pcs. 2x4 in. x 6 ft.; 12 pcs. 16 in. x 10 ft.; 24 pcs. 1x4 in. x 22 in.; 12 pcs. 1x4 in. x 17 in. 8-penny common nails.   □

This is a simple design for open shelves in a garage or other unfinished area. Simply nail *supports* (cleats) to the inside faces of wall studs and then nail boards on top of them. To keep balls and other items from falling off the shelves, nail 1×2s across the front faces. (See illustration on bottom of page 6)

These portable ladder shelves are easy to build in an afternoon. Modify dimensions to suit your needs in basements, garages, bedrooms, rumpus rooms, or other areas. The portability of this design is nice, especially when you need shelves in a particular location right away, but you don't want to have to decide now on the type of permanent storage you might want in that location. (See illustration on page 7)

Storage on hooks & in nooks

Some household objects are just too big to store in confined cupboards or cabinets. Items such as ladders, skis, and bicycles require special concern.

Heavy-duty hooks provide a simple means for storing a number of large or awkwardly shaped objects. Use a drill bit slightly smaller than the actual hook diameter to make pilot holes in studs, rafters, or joists. Then, just screw in the hooks. Use a tape measure to determine the dimensions of the items to be stored. Use those measurements to locate suitable storage areas. A tape measure should also be used to pinpoint exact hook placements so that each hook remains in line with others.

The person who first decided to put drawers in kitchen pantries should get a medal—what a great idea! Heavy-duty drawer guides support wide, short-sided drawers that slide out of pantries easily to offer a bird's-eye view of everything on them. Note that this bottom drawer offers lots of open space above so that it can hold large cereal boxes, blenders, and other tall items. The shelves above are adjustable to accommodate individual family needs.

Open areas under stairways offer homeowners many storage options (see chapter 5). Childrens' bedrooms almost never have enough storage capacity. Bunkbeds are a good choice when you want to add beds without losing floor space (see chapter 6).

Once you have decided on a storage project, you must take into account dimensional factors to ensure overall efficiency and convenience. Storage units should be sized to accommodate the items you intend to place in or on them. Also be sure that drawers, shelves, and counters are positioned for easy reach by those who will be using them. Use a tape measure to determine how high the kids can reach, for example. Countertops for adults are generally located 34 to 36 inches from the floor, but this may be too high for a children's play center.

When it comes time to drill holes in walls for shelf supports or cupboard installations, consider the household utilities that might be located inside the walls. Bathroom plumbing pipes are most often situated inside walls that rest behind toilets, sinks, and bathtub faucets. Always try to find and use studs as anchoring supports. If you must rely on wall anchors in lieu of studs, drill a shallow pilot hole through the wall surface and then probe through the opening with the end of a metal coat hanger or piece of wire. This will help you determine if pipes are in the way and if there is sufficient working room for anchoring devices.

Other home storage concerns

Laundry, utility, & storage room options

Along with efficient, convenient, and attractive storage components, laundry, utility, and dedicated storage rooms generally benefit from plenty of light and ventilation.

Windows provide fresh air ventilation to enclosed stale rooms. They also allow natural sunlight to brighten up otherwise dark spaces. Since you will want to install windows once and leave them in place forever, seriously consider top quality wood windows with excellent energy efficiency.

If your home storage project entails conversion of an attic space or remodeling of a vacated bedroom, don't overlook the benefits of skylights or ventilating roof windows.

Attic spaces become exceptionally hot in summer and quite damp in autumn and winter. If you use the attic for storage, consider installing an attic fan. This model from Leslie-Locke is equipped with a thermostat and humidistat. It will turn on automatically when temperatures exceed certain settings and when attic humidity exceeds preset limits.

There are no single answers for all home-storage concerns. Each family must decide how and where they want things stored so that their belongings remain safe and convenient.

Begin by talking about storage options with the rest of your family. Then, look through magazines and periodicals, visit model homes and home-improvement centers, and ask friends what they have done in their homes to solve similar storage problems. Good research should provide you with an abundance of practical, efficient, and attractive ideas.

Tools & materials

BUILDING efficient home-storage systems requires the use of numerous tools. Power tools can perform a great deal of work in little time. They can also allow for very precise and safe work as long as you adjust and operate them according to the manufacturers' recommendations, including the proper use of all safety guards and devices.

As your do-it-yourself skills improve, you might find yourself wanting to design and build higher quality projects utilizing fine cabinetmaking and woodworking techniques on higher grades of exotic, and more expensive, wood.

Expert cabinetmakers and woodworking artisans spend years learning their crafts. Like all novices, they started small and grew with time and practice. You must realize that building a beautiful armoire complete with dovetail joints, rail-and-stile panel doors, and ornate legs requires more than just a circular saw, hammer, and a few sheets of plywood.

Practice with your tools. Begin by building storage units that can teach you and your family useful skills and techniques. As your skills progress, study manuals on fine woodworking crafts before venturing into bigger and more intricate projects using materials of better quality.

Measuring tools

Every do-it-yourselfer must have a *tape measure*. It is one of the most common tools to be found in toolboxes and workshops. Stanley Powerlock models in 25- and 30-foot lengths are most versatile.

Along with a tape measure, you need a square. These tools allow users to draw straight lines, determine square corners, and more.

A large *framing square* rests behind a *Speed Square* on the left and a *combination square* on the right. Use the framing square to make straight 90-degree lines on plywood sections and wide

boards and to check for square corners on cabinets and large projects. The Speed Square includes embossed numbers that help determine angled end cuts. Its handy size is perfect for making straight lines on wood in preparation for cutting. The combination square features a sliding head that makes it easy to fit into smaller spaces.

Convenient tool accessories

Home-improvement centers, woodworking stores, and other do-it-yourself outlets are filled with tools. The Harbor Freight Tools catalog is filled with page after page of different tools. As you continue to expand your do-it-yourself activities, you will probably want to purchase more and more tools. Good-quality tools save time and help you build and finish projects with better results.

This handy spring-loaded device holds small finishing nails in place until a hammer tap or two starts them into the wood. It is a real finger and thumb saver and helps get small nails and brads started straight. (See illustration at top of next page.)

Nailing guns powered by compressed air are available in a variety of sizes and styles. Specific models are designed for different applications—16d nails for wood framing, roofing nails for shingles, staples for sheathing, and finishing nails for cabinetmaking. Since nail guns do not require a large amount of compressed air for their operation, small portable *air*

compressors like this are perfect. Small compressors can also be used for a wide range of other compressed air needs.

Saws

The 7¼-inch Makita *circular saw* in the back is flanked by a *cordless trim saw* on the left and a *cordless reciprocating saw* on the right. The large circular saw is perfect for cutting 2×4s, plywood, and other large boards. The smaller version works great for cutting small pieces of trim, paneling, countertops for sinks, and other intricate tasks. The reciprocating model is exceptionally handy in conditions where a circular saw cannot fit or operate safely. (See illustration at top of next page.)

Commonly referred to as a *chop saw*, this Makita slide compound saw quickly adjusts to cut wood in two different angles at the same time. This ability is perfect for molding and trim chores and other projects that require boards cut at specific angles. Its cutting unit slides back and forth, allowing it to cut boards as wide as 12 inches.

Table saws are found in almost every workshop. They are used for precision cutting. Saw blades adjust up and down to determine depths of cut and at angles to provide different degrees of cuts. This custom-made table saw cart rests on six locking casters and provides a large space inside for a dust-collection system. The cart's work surface is about ⅛ inch lower than the saw's table to ensure that wood slides easily onto the surface. The unit is also a handy workbench when the saw is not in operation.

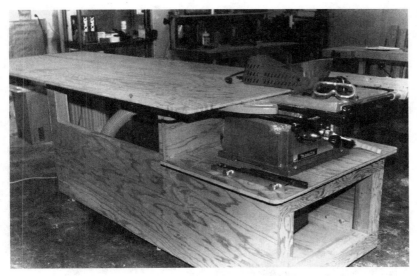

Table saws are equipped with *miter gauges*, which allow users to push smaller pieces of wood through saws at different angles. The end of the miter gauge on this Makita 10-inch table saw features a small block of wood secured in place. Brand new and never used, this piece of wood was a bit longer. Cut to this length, it now serves as a reference point to indicate exactly where the saw blade cuts.

Saw blades generally make clean, unsplintered cuts on only one board side. The blade enters the wood from one side for a clean cut and exits on the other side creating splinters. Circular saws cut from the bottom up (note the rotation arrow on the saw blade), so always place the good side of the wood down when using them. The opposite is true for table saws; they cut from the top down. Wood should be cut on a table saw with the good side up. This is especially important when cutting plywood and finished lumber for cabinet or cupboard trim.

Although full sheets of plywood can be cut on a table saw cart like the one on page 17, many do-it-yourselfers and professionals prefer to cut larger plywood panels with a circular saw and *cutting guide*. Four 2×4s rest on top of sturdy sawhorses. Two are located on the left side of the cut and two on the right side. The 2×4s support the entire plywood sheet through the total lengthwise cut.

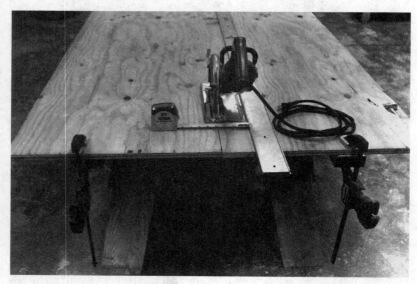

Notice that the all-purpose cutting guide is positioned a few inches to the right of the cut to compensate for the width of the saw's base plate. The blade is adjusted to a cutting depth about ¼ inch deeper than the thickness of the plywood. Quick-Grip *bar clamps* secure the plywood to the 2-x-4 supports.

A drill is needed to bore pilot holes for screws, access holes for anchors, and numerous other tasks. A good-quality ⅜-inch *power drill* is a good choice for most do-it-yourself needs. The ⅜-inch designation refers to the widest diameter drill bit shank that can fit into the drill's chuck. The Makita cordless *angle drill* on the left is very handy for drilling pilot holes for drawer guides in cabinet units and other occasions when holes must be drilled in confined spaces.

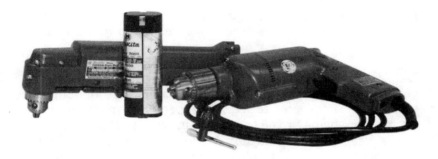

An assortment of good-quality wood-drilling and general purpose *bits* will serve you well. The *spade bits* on the left are designed for boring wide holes in wood. A set of heavy-duty black-oxide all-purpose *drill bits* are in the center. The *screw-sink* bits on the right are designed to drill pilot holes followed by wider openings to allow screws to either rest flush with or under surfaces. This process is referred to as a *countersink*.

The Makita ⅜-inch drill/driver is both a drill and a power screwdriver. The attachment secured in the drill chuck is called a *finder/driver*, and it works surprisingly well. A magnetic tip holds onto screws while a sleeve is  pulled over it to keep screws in place. As the screw begins to travel into the work, the sleeve slides back up toward the drill motor.

Drill/drivers are often equipped with a clutch mechanism. A collar located near the chuck rotates to adjust the amount of torque that is delivered to screws. Proper adjustment prevents screws from being driven too deeply into work. This feature works great for preventing damage to wood surfaces and from also stripping out screw holes in soft materials. One setting is designated specifically for drilling.

Routers, shapers, & trimmers

Home-storage projects can be built stronger and with more custom features by properly using routers, shapers, and trimmers. Routers and shapers use different bits to create a variety of grooves, curves, and other shapes on wood. Trimmers are used to cut holes in drywall, trim laminate countertops, and other such tasks. As with any power tool, be sure to follow all operating instructions. These tools rotate very sharp bits at such high speeds that the smallest error could result in damage to workpieces or personal injury.

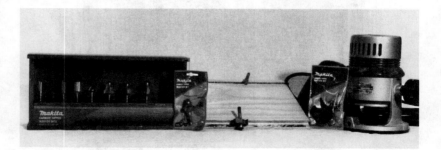

A set of *router bits* on the left is separated from the *router* on the right by a piece of plywood that has been rabbeted on the bottom and grooved on the top. A *rabbet* refers to a wood edge that has had a section cut out of its length. Another board fits into the rabbeted edge and can be glued and nailed or screwed to make a secure corner connection. A *groove* can also be used to join pieces of wood. Grooved sections are common on drawers to support drawer bottoms.

Routers can be operated accurately only with guides or templates. Adjustable guides are available that fit onto router bases, and you can use straight pieces of wood or all-purpose guides clamped in place. Since routers operate at such high speeds and cut wood so quickly, you must wear safety goggles and follow all operating instructions to the letter.

Shapers perform much the same functions as routers. They are designed with bits mounted on top, which makes it easy for users to watch their work progress. Heavy-duty motors are capable of cutting much more wood in a single pass. Shaper cutter heads are available in many different styles, and since shapers are so powerful, some cutter heads are designed to perform more than one cut in a single pass, such as simultaneously cutting a rabbet and rounding corners for cabinet-door edges.

Trimmers are available in corded and cordless models. They operate under the same basic principle as routers, using cutting bits that spin at a high speed. Designed mainly for trimming plastic laminate countertops, trimmers are also outfitted with special bits for cutting

out drywall sections. An assortment of attachments provides users with a multitude of trimming options at various angles.

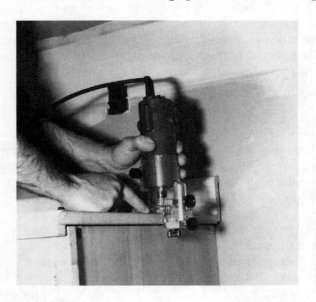

Accessory tools

Clamps help do-it-yourselfers and professional craftspeople in numerous ways. They can hold pieces of wood in place for cutting and keep glued sections together for curing. Quick-Grip bar clamps can be tightened and released with just one hand.

Attachments are available for holding corners together. Certain models are designed to push apart, rather than pulling together, which is great for loosening up and slowly separating glued pieces that must be taken apart for repair. Quick-Grip *spring clamps* are useful for a variety of smaller clamping tasks.

Sometimes you need to remove wood that cannot be cut accurately with a saw or other power tool, such as when you are setting door-handle throw plates or hinges. For those jobs, reach for a sharp *chisel*.

Planes are used to skim away layers of material on wood surfaces. They are designed to peel off layers of wood to render surfaces perfectly flat and even. *Hand planes* feature a flat bottom (shoe) with an adjustable cutting blade that projects out from the center. Set hand-plane blades to cut very thin layers of wood with each pass. If you try to cut too deeply with a hand plane, you are likely to dig in and mar surfaces.

The front shoe on this *power planer* is adjustable. When raised to expose more of the cutting blades, it cuts deeper. Notice that the back shoe rests at the same level as the cutting blades. As the power planer begins its trip over a wood edge, the cutting blades and back shoe are lower than the front shoe. Once blades make contact with wood, they cut away a layer leaving behind a smooth and flat surface for the back shoe to slide across.

Power planers are equipped with guides that must be properly adjusted to ensure accurate results. In addition, users must follow all operating instructions and wear safety goggles.

An orbital *sander* is shown here on the left, with a finishing sander in the middle and a cordless finishing sander on the right. The orbital model is much more powerful than the finishing sanders and removes a lot of material in a hurry. Use finishing sanders for final smoothing with light-grit sandpaper. Sandpaper is rated with numbers; the lowest numbers are coarser, the higher numbers finer. For initial, rough sanding, you might start with #100 and then finish with #240.

If you sand by hand, use a *sanding block* or at least wrap the sandpaper around a flat piece of wood. This guarantees that surfaces are sanded flat and even.

Cupboards and shelf supports that are expected to hold heavy objects securely must be mounted onto wall studs. The easiest way to locate studs is with a *stud finder*, a magnet attached to a rod that is enclosed in a case. When the magnet senses a drywall nail or screw just under the wall surface, its movement alerts the user to the presence of a stud.

Since light-switch and electrical-outlet boxes are almost always nailed to wall studs, start hunting for studs on either side of them. Once you find a stud, measure over 16 inches and use the stud finder to locate the next stud. Studs are commonly positioned on 16-inch centers.

You will need nails and screws for almost every storage project. Nails are calibrated by number; 16d (16 penny) nails are about 3½ inches long and are used mostly for framing walls. Eight-penny nails are about half as long. Finishing nails have very small heads, which allows them to be set easily; that is, they can be driven just under wood surfaces to create small pockets that can be filled with putty and sanded smooth to hide them.

Securing lightweight shelf units and other objects to walls between studs requires special anchors. A variety of styles are available. The large bodied model on the left is simply screwed into drywall; no pilot hole is required. Once secure, a separate screw is twisted into it.

The two anchors in the middle require pilot holes of the specific size recommended on the label. They are pushed into the hole and then filled with a screw, which spreads the anchor body and holds the screw securely.

Materials

The anchor body at the top is designed to be inserted with a hammer. Inserting the screw then compresses the body against the inside face of the wall.

Plywood is available in thicknesses from ⅛ inch to 1¼ inches. Most general-purpose plywood is made of fir, sometimes with innerplies of pine. You can also purchase plywood with outer plies of birch, oak, and other hardwoods.

Plywood grades are designated by letters, with A being the smoothest and most attractive. Most sheets carry a two letter rating; A/C plywood has one A side and one C side. D is the lowest rating and frequently has shallow knotholes and other imperfections. (See illustration at top of next page.)

Hardwood plywood, like this sheet of birch, is generally rated A/B or A/A. Since these sheets are made from hardwood, mills make sure that both sides are finished smooth and without obvious flaws. Hardwood plywood is an excellent material to use when building nice cupboards, cabinets, bookcases, and other creative indoor storage pieces.

When you cut plywood, you might notice open knotholes between plies. These gaps can be filled with putty and sanded or covered with trim. If you notice that the plies have begun to separate, use a thin piece of wood to spread wood glue over the loosened plies and then clamp them together using blocks and clamps.

DAP offers a number of different kinds of glue designed for a variety of applications. Weldwood Carpenter's Glue does an

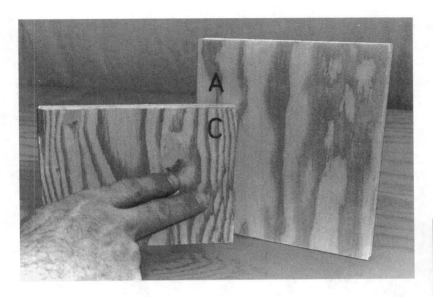

excellent job of holding pieces of wood together. Glue every wood joint and then use finishing nails or wood screws for extra security. Use Wood Dough and Finishing Putty to finish trim pieces, Vinyl Spackling for holes in drywall, and Contact Cement to secure materials other than wood. (See illustration at top of next page.)

Most home-improvement projects require stain or paint to make them look finished. Behr offers stain and paint products for all occasions, in standard and custom-made colors. To ensure a good stain or paint finish, be sure to read and follow all application instructions. (See illustration at middle of next page.)

Improperly prepared surfaces do not accept stain and paint as well as you might expect. Bare surfaces should be coated with a sealer or primer first to guarantee best results. Victor Lopez, technical service manager for Behr, says that almost 95 percent of all stain and paint problems are a direct result of users not following application instructions.

Building and installing home-storage units can create quite a pile of sawdust, wood shavings, and other debris. Make your

cleaning tasks easier by using efficient tools. Empire brush offers an extra-large dustpan called the Dirt Catcher Pan that scoops up large piles of sawdust and wood scraps. Foxtail and whisk brooms do a good job of sweeping up even the smallest remnants of dust and dirt.

Simple storage-unit construction

SIMPLE construction of a home-storage project does not mean sloppy construction. Rather, it refers to units that can be put together utilizing relatively simple skills and standard, less-costly materials. The basic differences between an expensive bookcase and a generic shelving unit are the amount and style of their trim and molding pieces, the types of woodworking joints and level of craft skills employed, and the quality of materials used in their assembly.

All home-storage projects should be constructed square, plumb, and perpendicular. Joints must be solidly glued and reinforced with nails or screws. Units should offer sturdy, convenient, and efficient storage; not flimsy, hard-to-reach, inadequately supported accidents waiting to happen.

Practical installations

A set of metal angle brackets, properly installed, can support a shelf just as well as ornate wooden brackets. Metal brackets are fine in a garage or utility room, but not in an attractive and well-furnished living room. Neither type will work at all, however, if they are installed off level.

The bracket on the right was installed first at a specified height. One end of a 4-foot level rests on top of the secured bracket while the loose bracket on the left is maneuvered into a position perfectly level with it. One screw is driven to secure the loose bracket to the wall, level with the first bracket. A smaller level is then used to ensure that the brackets are mounted vertically plumb before additional screws are inserted to complete the installation. (See illustration at top of next page.)

Brackets that are expected to support shelves that, in turn, need to support heavy loads must be secured to wall studs. Anchors designed for between-stud applications, which are

secured only to the drywall, do not offer nearly the same degree of solid support.

Stud finders are designed to pinpoint the location of nails or screws employed to secure drywall to studs. Notice how the stud-finder magnet rests horizontally when positioned over a screw or nail. After locating the stud nearest to where you want to locate a bracket, drive a slender nail into the wall at that point. Once the nail penetrates drywall, it should offer resistance as it comes in contact with the stud. Should the nail pass easily into the wall without resistance, you missed the stud. Move the nail about ¾ inch left or right and try again.

One of the easiest and quickest ways to provide a room with shelves is to purchase a prefabricated shelving unit.

This versatile shelf system is lightweight, sturdy, and economical. Shelves rising more than about 3 feet from the floor should be secured to walls to keep them from falling over.

A simple plywood shelf features two sides, a top, bottom, and shelves all cut to the same width. First determine what you want to store in the unit, then space the shelves accordingly. Indicate the locations of shelves with marks on the side panels. Then use a framing square to make long, straight lines across side panels to identify shelf positions. For this application, 2½-inch finishing nails were driven through the side panels, into the shelves.

Narrow boards are attached to the panels at the back and below shelves with 2½-inch finishing nails. Then, drive screws

Simple storage-unit construction   31

through these boards, into wall studs to support the unit. Each unit should be equipped with at least two such rail supports.

Long, straight lines on the inside face of side panels serve as guides to ensure that the shelves are nailed into correct positions. Use a framing square and pencil to make light lines on the panels. Another line on the outside of the panel can indicate where to start the nails so that they go directly into the centers of shelf boards.

Improved simple shelving units

Plywood shelves nailed to side panels offer adequate basic storage. However, such simple designs cannot be expected to support great amounts of weight. After all, the only fasteners holding these units together are finishing nails.

A more secure and sturdy method of constructing simple plywood storage units involves grooves (dadoes) and rabbets. Mark the side panels as before. Then clamp both panels to a workbench with the pencil marks perfectly aligned. Use a ¾-inch router bit to cut a ¾-inch-wide and ⅜-inch-deep groove along the lines. Shelves can then be glued and nailed into the grooves.

Note the straight 2×4 that serves as a router guide. It is positioned to the side of the groove at a distance equal to the space between the edge of the router bit and far edge of the router's base. Make a few test cuts on some scrap wood first to ensure that your measurements are accurate. Grooves and rabbets are commonly cut to half the thickness of the piece that will fit into them.

Spread wood glue thoroughly around grooves and on shelf edges, clamp them together securely, and then nail or screw the pieces together. Drywall screws are used for this unit

for added strength. They can be covered up with a section of pegboard, which we will discuss on page 35.

Attach the mounting support boards to the shelves with glue and nails or screws. Note that the top of this unit fits into a rabbet along the top edge of the side panel. A rabbet is basically the same as a groove except that it is cut along the outer edge rather than in a center section.

Dress up the front edges of simple plywood shelf units with pieces of trim or molding. The molding across the top features a lipped pattern, while the trim running down the side is flat. Home-improvement centers and lumberyards offer a wide variety of trim and molding styles. Select those that most satisfy your taste in widths that match your work—¾ inch wide for this application.

This shelving unit can be mounted in an open location with its sides conveniently exposed. Pegboard can be attached to the sides to offer additional storage. (See margin art.)

Pegboard must be installed at least ¼ inch away from walls or any other surface to leave room for the insertion of hooks. Therefore, install *furring strips* over the screws on side panels with small 4d finishing nails driven through panels and into shelves.

Cut the pegboard to the same dimensions as the side panels, and then attach it with screws driven through the furring strips and into the shelves. (See illustration at bottom left.)

The addition of furring strips and pegboard to these side panels makes it impossible for ¾-inch trim or molding to cover the front edges. Instead, use 1×2s for trim, secured with 1¾-inch finishing nails. Use a *nail set* to drive the nail heads just below the surface and then fill the small pockets with wood dough or putty. (See illustration at bottom right.)

Customizing simple shelving units

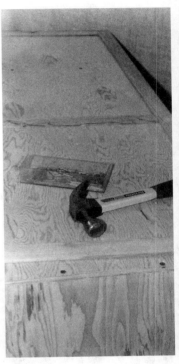

Another way to hide nails after they have been set is to fill the pockets with glue, wipe off the excess with a damp rag, and then let it cure for about a minute. Sand surfaces with medium (100 grit) or fine (240 grit) sandpaper.

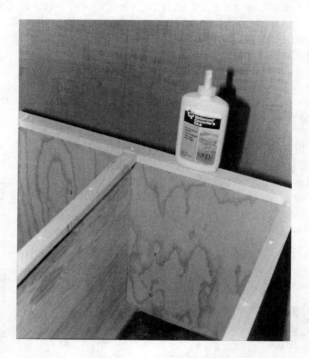

Mix sanding dust with glue to fill nail-set pockets if you want to more closely match the color of the surrounding wood. Professional cabinetmakers and woodworkers employ this technique only on rare occasions, preferring to use wood dough or putty for expert results on fine pieces. The sawdust-glue mix is useful, however, on basic projects intended for everyday use or simple storage.

Use a power planer to even up and match the bottom and side trim pieces. The bottom piece was about ⅛ inch too wide for this application. Whenever using a power or hand plane, you must be certain that the workpiece is free from all nails, screws, or other debris. Hard objects can chip planer blades and render them relatively useless. Be sure to wear safety goggles, too.

Along with providing a place to hang a workshop apron, wallpapering tools, and cleaning utensils, this solid shelf unit can easily support heavy objects. It is also more attractive than the simple unit that is nailed together without trim.

Jim Yocum is nailing trim to the face of a large 4-foot-wide-x-7-foot-tall garden-tool storage unit that was built in the same fashion as the smaller one just described. It rests on its backside to accommodate easy assembly. A piece of hardboard has been nailed to the rear of the unit to provide a solid back and to keep the unit square. A single shelf is located about 2½ feet from the top and is inserted into grooves on both side panels. The top and bottom sections fit into rabbets. (See illustration at top of next page.)

Simple storage-unit construction   37

Additional shelf-unit designs

Storage units featuring solidly affixed shelves offer ideal solutions to many home-storage problems. However, there are occasions when adjustable shelves would be better; for example, on units for living or family rooms where framed pictures, awards, and other objects are rearranged from time to time, or bathrooms to accommodate varying sizes of toiletry containers.

A series of aligned holes drilled part way into each side of this shelf panel hold special shelf brackets. Be sure to drill the holes on a level horizontal plane to ensure that the shelves rest flat and level. (See illustration at left.)

Do-it-yourselfers can spend a lot of time accurately marking positions for drilling holes for shelf brackets. Using a *drill press* would help to keep each hole straight. A simple method for aligning the holes is to use a small section of pegboard as a template. Be certain that one corner of the pegboard panel is square and is used for alignment each time.

A pegboard template can help you to drill straight holes into wood panels. Use a piece of masking tape on the drill bit to mark the depth of your holes.

Another method of building adjustable shelving units is to use notched metal supports that hold special brackets. The metal supports on this side panel have been inserted into grooves made by a *dado assembly* on a table saw. Note the ¾-inch groove at the bottom of the panel into which the unit's bottom piece can fit.

A ¾-inch straight router bit was used to make the rabbet on the top of this side panel. A ⅜-inch rabbet bit could have also been used. Regardless of the bit you use, always test your router's

cutting width and depth on a piece of scrap wood, adjusting the guide and cutting depth until you are satisfied. Note the router guide attached to the base of this tool. (See illustration at left.)

Grooves for these shelf supports could have been made with a straight router bit. However, the supports were a bit wider than ⅝ inch, and a straight router bit of the exact size was not available. This Makita dado set includes a number of ⅛-inch-wide cutters, one ¹⁄₁₆-inch-wide cutter, and a couple of thin paper washers. Adding two paper washers to the blades allowed it to cut a groove slightly wider than ⅝ inch, into which the shelf support fit perfectly.

A metal shelf support is positioned next to the dado set as a gauge to accurately adjust the dado cutting depth. Dado blades and cutters must be installed according to the manufacturer's directions to achieve safe and satisfactory results. Always be certain to disconnect the table saw from its power source before attempting to change blades. (See illustration at left.)

A piece of scrap wood was used to test the accuracy of the dado blade's width and depth of cut. The dado cut was stopped just short of the ¾-inch bottom groove. A sharp wood chisel was used to clean out the uncut portions of the dado next to the groove. (See illustration at top of next page.)

This metal shelf support is embossed with numbers on its face. These are used as guides to ensure that supports are installed evenly on shelf unit panels so that their brackets are installed level with each other.

The lid on this unit has been glued and nailed into rabbets located at the tops of side panels. The bottom was glued and nailed into grooves. Here, 1-x-2 trim pieces are being glued and nailed to the front face. A Campbell Hausfeld finishing nailer made the job easy. Note the two wall-mounting support boards resting horizontally inside. They can be secured with glue and pins from the finishing nailer.

Two or more shelves fit easily in this adjustable shelf unit. Packages of shelf brackets, complete with brads or screws, are commonly available at home-improvement centers, lumberyards, and hardware stores. (See illustration at top of next page.)

Drawer basics

Most drawers are simply shallow boxes equipped with guides and then adorned with a separate front panel.

Notice the shallow rabbet joint at the front of this drawer. Front and side pieces were secured with glue and staples. The screw that is visible on the inside face of the drawer is one of four screws that hold the front face panel in place. (See illustration at top of next page.)

Drawer guides are available in a variety of styles, sizes, and price ranges. Those outfitted with rollers generally slide and operate easiest. A drawer guide section has been screwed to the

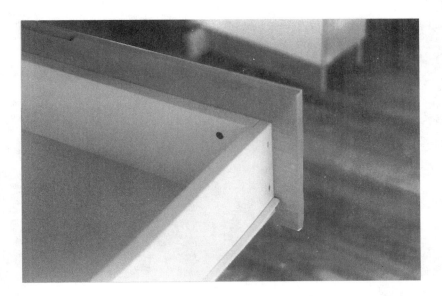

lower side edge of this drawer and can fit into a matching section attached to the inside of its host cabinet. Be sure to follow all instructions included with drawer guides. Pay strict attention to all dimensional recommendations to ensure accurate, easy drawer operation. See chapter 8 for more information on drawer construction.

Simple storage-unit construction 43

Garages, basements, & attics

ALTHOUGH HOME garages are designed for automobile storage, it doesn't take long for them to become storage depots for a variety of household belongings. This phenomenon makes one wonder just how many garages are filled with actual automobiles?

Basements can be outfitted with sufficient cupboards, cabinets, and shelves to accommodate a great deal of family belongings. Although access might limit the actual size of objects to be stored there, basements generally offer lots of wide open room for storage.

Many older homes feature steep-pitched rafter-constructed roofs, as opposed to many newer homes with roofs made with prefabricated trusses. *Rafter-roofs* frequently result in wide open attic areas with steep pitches affording lots of head room. Attics like this offer plentiful storage options. On the other hand, prefabricated trusses are not designed to support attic storage.

Trusses are constructed with dimensional lumber that is smaller than most wood used for rafter roofs. They rely on gusset plates and engineered designs for strength. Certain truss designs that incorporate attic-storage features require larger dimensional lumber and more supports. Hence, they cost more than regular roof trusses.

This is not to say that regular trusses are incapable of supporting any storage. Some lightweight storage, like Christmas decorations, boxes of memories, and other small objects, might be acceptable when interior house walls serve as truss supports. If you have any questions about attic storage in homes featuring roof trusses, call a local truss manufacturer for definitive information.

Garage storage

It doesn't take long to fill a garage with discarded toys, boxes of outgrown clothes, bicycle parts, and so on. In addition, do-it-yourselfers frequently need space to store odds and ends left over from other home-improvement projects.

Admittedly not pleasant to look at, this simple ceiling rack constructed of 2×4s nailed to joists above that support other 2×4s nailed to them provides storage for pieces of lumber, trim, and other long, slender objects. The shelves in the background could be equipped with doors to conceal their contents.

Heavy-duty hooks screwed into ceiling joists offer a sturdy means of supporting objects from a garage ceiling. Hooks like this one might be perfect when secured to header beams located on walls directly above garage doors. Garages with high ceilings generally feature wide open spaces above garage doors where hooks or shelves could provide additional and out-of-the-way storage. (See illustration at top of next page.)

Ladders, especially long extension ladders, pose unique storage problems. Heavy-duty hooks mounted to walls work great, but they take up a lot of wall space. With the right hooks, you might be able to store ladders along a section of the garage ceiling. Be certain that the hooks you employ for such a ceiling mount are designed with arms to prevent the ladder from slipping off accidentally.

Garages located under living spaces sometimes offer hidden storage space between ceiling/floor joists. Before cutting away the ⅝-inch drywall, which is required between garages and living spaces, determine the locations of heat ducts and plumbing pipes above by sketching a floor plan of the room or rooms above the garage. Include exact locations of bathroom fixtures and heat registers. Use that sketch and its measurements in the garage as a guide to determine where such utilities might be found, so that you can avoid them. (See illustration at top of next page.)

Once you have successfully located and opened up an unobstructed section between ceiling/floor joists, cover the top and sides with ⅝-inch drywall. This can serve as the fire protection that is required by building and fire codes. With drywall installed and finished, mount boards along the bottom edge to serve as storage supports. They can be toenailed or screwed in place.

Basement ceilings also offer options for storage. Again, you must determine the locations of heat ducts and plumbing pipes to avoid unnecessary drywall removal. About the only drawbacks to this type of ceiling storage are the possible loss of some insulation and the chance that you might find the storage unsightly, especially in a finished basement.

For finished basements equipped with heat that pose no unusual problems with regard to insulation loss, consider installing a box inside ceiling/floor joist spaces in lieu of simple board supports. One end of the box can be secured to the space with a hinge, and the free end held closed with twisting blocks or heavy-duty throw locks. Rope or chain can be attached to joists above and the box's free end to hold the unit in place when it is lowered. Paint the bottom of the box to match the ceiling.

This open basement-storage unit is 8 feet wide, 8 feet tall, and 1 foot deep. It consists of two sheets of ¾-inch A/C plywood for the top, bottom, sides, center panel, and shelves; two sheets of ¼-inch hardboard for the back; and two 8-foot 2×4s for the front and rear floor supports, with five shorter 2×4s spaced equally and perpendicular to them. (See illustration at top of next page.)

Units like this can be made in any dimension desired. However, when shelves span distances greater than 36 inches, they should have vertical supports in the middle to prevent sagging.

The 8-foot-long plywood shelves for this unit feature ⅛-inch-deep grooves cut with a ¾-inch router bit to keep the four 2-foot vertical supports solidly in position. This allowed the shelves to be a full 8 feet long for added strength. In my experience, 8-foot-long shelves with vertical supports in the middle do not sag as much as 4-foot-long shelves without midspan support. (See illustration at top of next page.)

Locating space and designing storage units for basements should not be difficult. In open basements, a large storage unit can be located in the middle of the room as long as it is secured to joists above with screws. Build two of them back to back and outfit them with doors to serve as storage and room-dividing partitions.

Keep storage away from furnaces, electrical panels, and other utilities. In an unfinished basement, be sure that walls are sealed to prevent moisture penetration. If water accumulation and high humidity are problems, correct them with exterior footing drains and then line interior basement walls with sheets of plastic to prevent recurring moisture accumulation.

Attic storage

As previously mentioned, attics can serve as excellent home-storage depots, but homeowners must be aware of the weight limitations for prefabricated trusses. It is common to see construction workers weighing more than 200 pounds walking around on horizontal truss members during their installation. However, prolonged storage of items weighing 25 to 200 pounds on unsupported truss members (that is, with no interior house wall underneath) can create trouble.

This open attic space was created by the construction of a custom hip roof. There is a floor to ceiling space of about 7 feet in the center of the attic with head room diminishing rapidly as the roof runs down to the walls. A regular closet has been

framed in this section of the attic with an additional crawl-space access hole added behind. Since the crawl space is so small, storage is limited to little-used items. Lights and light switches are provided for the closet and crawl space.

Stick-framed roofs (those with separate rafters) are constructed with bigger material, typically 2×6s or 2×8s. They also include large ceiling joists that run from the top of one exterior wall to the other as a means of providing roof strength and a ceiling for rooms below. Their design allows for heavier attic storage, especially when interior house walls serve as supports.

Walking around in unfinished attics poses some hazards. An unfinished attic floor generally consists of 2-×-6 or larger ceiling joists running 16 or 24 inches on center with insulation between them. The only thing holding up the insulation is drywall. Step on the insulation and you are likely to go right through the drywall. So walk on the top of the ceiling joists only; do not step in between them.

Also be aware of nails protruding through roof sheathing and into attic spaces. These nails secure the roofing material and can be hard to see in a darkened attic. Keep your head away from the attic ceiling.

An easy way to gain access to attic spaces is to install an attic stairway. Units like this generally sell for around $60 and are easy to install. They are easiest to put in before insulation and drywall have been installed, such as in a new house or a new addition.

Position an attic stairway in a location that allows for convenient access; like in a garage, rumpus or family room, or wide hallway. In addition, be sure to place attic stairways close to the center of your home's roof line or where the attic offers its greatest head room.

Once an appropriate location has been selected for an attic stairway, inspect the attic to be certain ceiling joists run parallel with your intended access opening. Ceiling joists should not be cut to facilitate attic stairway installations, and prefabricated roof trusses cannot be cut for such purposes.

Attic stairway installation instructions are easy to comprehend and follow. Once an opening has been made, nail up 1×4s along each side of the opening. Position them about ¾ inch inside the joist opening to which the stairway will be secured. These 1×4s will support the stairway in place while you nail its frame to the joists.

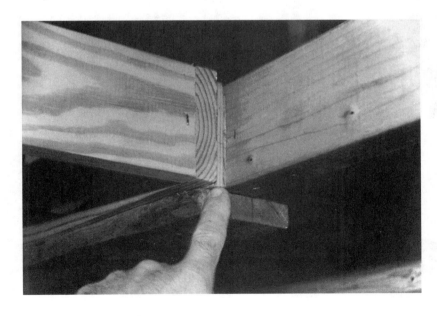

To ensure that the 1×4s are located properly, measure the width of the attic stairway and compare it with the opening between joists. The 1×4s must extend in far enough to support the stairway's outer frame on both sides while allowing the stairs to be pulled down into an operating position. Note that a section of ½-inch plywood serves as a shim between the stairway frame and joist.

With the 1×4s nailed in place, open the attic stairway to gain access to its frame. Sixteen-penny nails are used to secure the frame to ceiling joists according to directions.

Once the stairway has been securely nailed to the ceiling joists, open it all the way in preparation for cutting bottom sections flush with the floor. (See illustration at top of next page.)

Following directions, fold back the lowest stairway section and measure along the front of the rail; note the distance from the floor to the edge of the rail. Then make the same measurement on the back side of the rail; it will be shorter than the front. Repeat this on the other rail. (See illustration at bottom of next page.)

If you followed directions carefully and made accurate cuts on the rail ends, your attic stairway should meet flush with the floor for a perfect fit.

An interior wall will be installed in the middle of this room. It will serve as a room divider and also as a support for the roof trusses. The bottom of the attic stairway will then be sealed and painted to match the new ceiling.

Owens-Corning R-30 insulation rises from the drywall ceiling below to a height of about 9½ inches. A small, narrow pathway is built out of 2×4s and ¾-inch C/D plywood to facilitate walking in the storage section safely. The platform is located about 3 inches above the insulation.

While working to make your attic a suitable storage space, consider installing a few lights, with the switch mounted next to the attic stairway. This extra effort will make it much easier to find things in the storage area.

General home-storage options

CUPBOARDS, cabinets, and shelves are common items for home storage. Most of our belongings rest on shelves of some type, but these units are not the only options available to store household goods.

Many homeowners rely on different storage accessories to accommodate their everyday needs. With a little imagination, these alternatives can be made to facilitate even greater and more organized home storage.

How many homes have at least one small closet that looks like this? It doesn't take long for an accumulation of stuff to fill such spaces, especially for busy families always on the go.

A few shelves strategically placed in small broom closets can turn them into organized and convenient storage spaces. A decision to organize a closet like this can also present you with a perfect opportunity to get rid of a lot of junk that has been tossed into it and is no longer needed or wanted.

Installing shelves in an enclosed broom closet is easy. Small 1×2s can be nailed to studs to serve as shelf supports. In shallow closets, these boards might have to run from the back all the way to the front in order for them to be secured to studs. Determine how high you want the shelves, then secure the end of one board to a stud. Use a level to position the other board end so that your shelves will be flat. (See illustration at top of next page.)

Broom closet

In this closet, a stud is located in the center, between the side walls, and the shelves were maintained at a narrow depth to provide room in front for a vacuum cleaner. The existing longer shelf supports located about 5 feet up from the floor were equipped with special hooks for a broom and mop. Notice that the shelves located close to the top of the closet are narrow to make it easier to reach items on them.

Hanging things

Household goods often are hung from nails partially driven into pieces of wood. Although such a simple rack might serve a useful purpose, you must admit that it leaves much to be desired in the way of visual attractiveness. (See illustration at top of next page.)

Many people dislike using pegboard for household storage because the hooks often fall off when items are removed from them. Sta-Put Color Pegs won't fall off, and they make pegboard a much more acceptable means of storage.

Pegboard must be mounted on furring strips to provide maneuvering room for hooks. Here, 1½-inch-×-½-inch-×-4-foot long strips cut from a 2×4 on a table saw are securely anchored to studs with drywall screws.

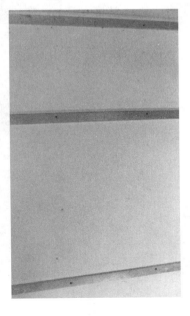

Dark screw heads indicate the location of a furring strip behind this pegboard. The screws must be driven through furring strips and into wall studs. Although pegboard is available in ⅛-inch-thick sheets, ¼-inch sheets are much sturdier. (See illustration at top of next page.)

This wall-storage system looks neat and it holds much more than that piece of wood with nails in it. Notice the handy hooks used to support brooms, a shovel, rake, and pitchfork. Sta-Put Color Pegs support everything else.

Broom handle hooks are available in a few different styles, with some capable of supporting more weight than others. When not in use, these models simply fold down flat. Be sure to secure them with screws driven through the pegboard and furring strips and into studs. (See illustration at right.)

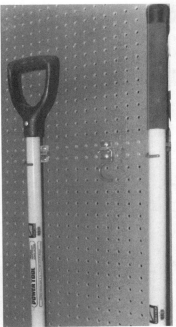

This is another type of broom/mop support mechanism. The handles are secured by pushing them through from the bottom. The weight causes a rubber lever to close down on handles and wedge them in place.

Laundry and utility rooms, workshops, and garages often have open space above windows that can be ideal places to store small items. A small piece of trim has been nailed to the edge of this shelf to form a lip that keeps items from falling off. The shelf is supported by a Simpson Strong-Tie bracket installed upside down.

Three ¾-inch screws secure this bracket to the shelf. Since a full-sized header beam occupies the entire space above the window, little concern was given to finding a stud and positioning the bracket on the shelf accordingly. Not all metal brackets can be installed in this upside down fashion, as some will bend and fail. This style, however, features a bar that connects both ends of the bracket for maximum support and holding strength.

Laundry & utility rooms

Laundry and utility rooms are frequently used as sewing centers, and sewing requires numerous small parts, bobbins, spools, and tools. Creating storage for these small items can present a challenge. Here, ¼-inch pegboard and Sta-Put Color Pegs create an efficient and convenient solution. Sta-Put pegs are available in three different shapes to securely store a multitude of sewing items.

Another common storage problem in laundry and utility rooms involves coat hangers. A simple solution is to use a section of closet rod (wood dowel) secured under a cupboard. Alternatively, consider installing a long towel rack under a cupboard or shelf.

Some cupboard and cabinet doors made of plywood or featuring solid rails and stiles can be outfitted with pegboard to increase storage space. A small shelf with a lip in front could also be installed on the door to hold small items. In the kitchen, door shelves can store packages of soup mix, recipes, and other lightweight items. (See illustration below.)

As with all other pegboard applications, an open space must be maintained behind to accommodate hooks. When installing furring strips, be certain to use short screws that will not penetrate through doors. (See illustration at right.)

There are times when open, adjustable shelves are preferable to fixed, closed shelves. They offer more flexibility and convenience.

Shelves

This metal support is similar to the one presented earlier except that the notches in it are vertical, not horizontal. The special brackets for this type of support are available in different colors. (See illustration at top of next page.)

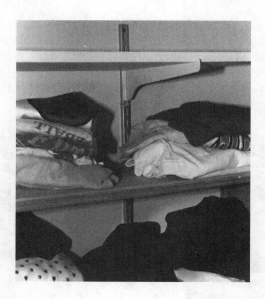

These types of shelving brackets make ideal storage units for glassware, especially when you use glass shelves. This application includes two metal support brackets with a wide mirror between them, two narrow mirrors on each side, and a light above to enhance the overall effect.

An attractive coat and hat rack located in a utility room, front-door entrance, or back-door hallway can be very convenient. During wet or snowy winter months you might really appreciate the ability to let wet coats and other garments drip dry.

A wood plug placed over a mounting screw can be cut with a finishing saw and then sanded to completely hide the screw head. Styled hardwood pegs are inexpensive and commonly available at home-improvement centers and craft stores. You can make them yourself with a lathe. Mount them on a piece of oak or other exotic wood and you'll have an attractive and efficient rack for many applications. These simple racks also work well for hanging bathrobes or pajamas in bathrooms, baseball caps in bedrooms, and coffee mugs in kitchens.

In preparation for router work, a piece of oak is secured between dogs inserted into a woodworker's workbench and woodworking vise. The router bit selected made an attractive lipped edge on the board. The workpiece must be solidly secured before routing. In addition, users must wear safety goggles and a dust mask. (See illustration at top of next page.)

A tape measure, combination square, and pencil are used to designate the center of the board, and a series of marks indicate the evenly spaced locations of the pegs. (See illustration at middle of next page.)

Once you determine the center of the board, adjust a combination square to that point. Then, holding a pencil at the end of the square, slide the square and pencil carefully along

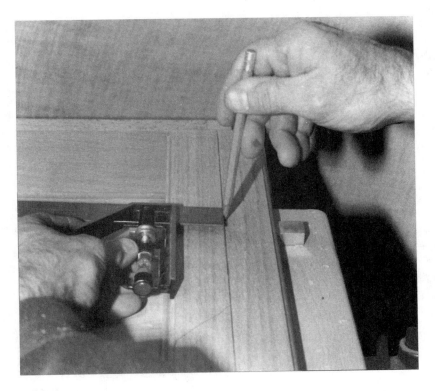

the edge of the board. This technique should assure you of a straight and accurate center line. (See illustration above.)

A drill press is set to bore holes to the necessary depth. Clamps secure the workpiece and underlying boards to the drill-press table. A spade bit is used since the holes aren't too deep. The tip of this spade bit will not bore deep enough to penetrate the entire board.

The hole on the right will support a hardwood peg. The hole on the left was drilled with a countersink drill bit that made a pilot hole for the mounting screw and also provided a wide opening for the screw head that will be covered with a plug. If mounting holes line up with studs, wood screws are employed for the installation. If studs aren't conveniently located, use drywall anchors, as seen here on the right. (See illustration at top of next page.)

Wood plugs can be cut from similar material to cover mounting screws and make storage racks appear more finished. Plug Cutter bits are designed for use with drill presses exclusively; you cannot use them with hand-held power drills. Once the plugs are cut to depth, use a slender screwdriver to break them loose from the board.

After the edges have been routed and all the holes have been drilled, use wood glue to secure pegs. Use a sliver of wood to help spread glue completely around peg holes. Push the pegs into position and then twist them ¼ turn to ensure that they are well seated with plenty of glue surrounding the entire opening. Wipe off excess glue that seeps out of openings with a damp rag. (See illustration at top of next page.)

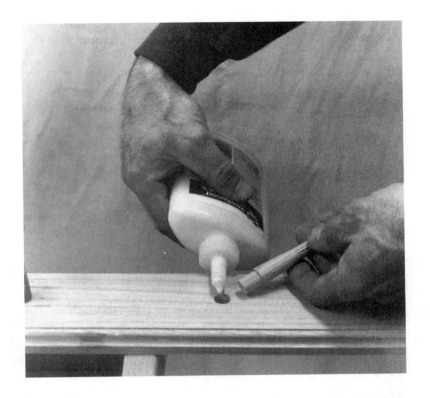

Fireplace mantels provide shelf space suitable for a variety of display items. Mantels can be supported by brackets secured to walls and positioned on each side of a fireplace opening. They can also be attached to wall studs and blocks.

Fireplace mantels

Note the slight indentation between the insulation and top of the exposed fireplace brick. This will be filled with a 1½-inch mantel made of clear Douglas fir.

The Douglas fir is cut to fit the mantel opening. The edges have been rounded off with a router. Wood screws are driven through the framing block into the mantel to secure it in place. Notice the bricks extending underneath, which serve as additional mantel supports. A level ensures that the mantel is perfectly horizontal. Use shims under the mantel if necessary to level it.

Although some homeowners would prefer to stain such a nice piece of Douglas fir, this homeowner chose to paint hers white. The mantel is solidly secured and is capable of supporting just about anything that is likely to be placed upon it. (See illustration at top of next page.)

Stairways are integral parts of all homes with basements or second floors. Their common design almost always allows for storage space beneath them. Some homebuilders simply enclose those spaces with studs and drywall, ignoring the potential for increased home storage. If your home features a stairway with no open space below, cut out a section of drywall and poke a drop light or flashlight into the opening to see if storage space is available.

This open, unused space near the furnace has been turned into a closet area. A 1-x-4 block mounted on the wall supports a closet rod that supports out-of-season clothes. A chain hanging from the rod supports another closet rod for even more clothes. In the background, an angled door leads to an under-stairway storage area where seldom used items are kept. (See illustration at bottom of page 71.)

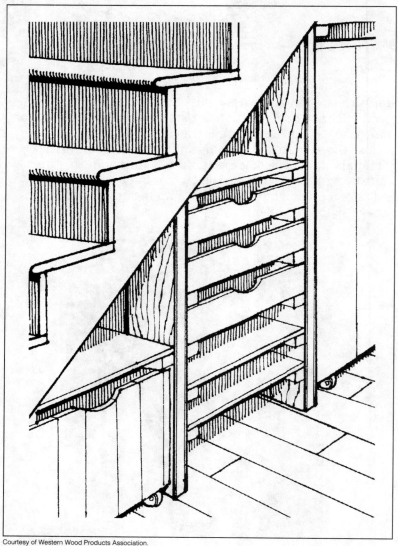

Courtesy of Western Wood Products Association.

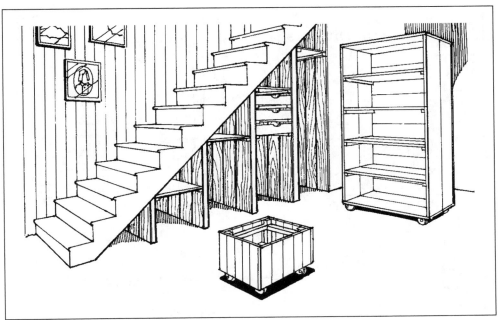

These projects from the Western Wood Products Association
provide excellent means of utilizing otherwise wasted space
under an exposed home stairway. Take your time to make
accurate measurements and be careful to make precise angled
cuts. Once a unit has been installed, fill all nail sets with wood
dough or putty, sand to perfection, and finish with a good-
quality Behr sealer and stain or paint. Plans for a variety of
such projects are available from the WWPA at a very
economical price. (See illustrations at bottom of preceeding
page and at the top of this page. Also see plans on pages 74–76.)

Framework/Dividers

Fig. 1

Lay out divider wall spacing on floor, allowing a 24-inch inside measurement between dividers plus 2½ inches for thickness of finished wall. Then, using a plumb line, mark the underside of stairs directly above floor spacing.

Fig. 4

A

Transfer angle to 2x4 frame top (A) and rip to angle (cut board lengthwise). Before installing, assemble entire divider wall, including frame (angled top, bottom, sides, center supports) and paneling. Move finished wall into position and glue/nail bottom frame to floor. Attach angled top frame to underside of stairs with nails or screws. Make sure fasteners are long enough to go through covering and into stringers.

Fig. 2

C

J

B

A

If stair stringers are exposed, attach 2x2 bottom frame (A) to wood floor with glue and nails; if floor is concrete, use tile mastic and/or concrete nails. Glue/nail vertical 2x2 supports (B) to stair stringers and floor frame.

Glue/nail horizontal 2x2s (C) between supports at top. Where span is more than 36 inches, add horizontal center support (D).

Apply paneling boards to one or both sides of frame.

If stair stringers are enclosed with drywall, plaster or paneling, locate position of stringer just as you would find studs in an existing wall: use magnetic stud finder; look for drywall nailing pattern, or "sound" them out by gently tapping with a hammer.

Fig. 3

Determine stair angle by placing a piece of cardboard vertically where stair angle meets the floor. Make sure one side of cardboard is square to floor, then reach inside with a pencil and mark floor/stringer angle on cardboard.

Pull-out Storage Bin

19"x 21" x 15" high, plus casters

MATERIALS LIST
A — Bottom frame:
  2x2s: (2) 16-½''; (2) 17-½ "
B — Corner posts:
  2x2s: (4) 12-¾"
C — Bottom boards:
  1x4's: (5) 19-½ "
D — Top frame:
  2x2s: (2) 16-½''; (2) 14-½"
E — Sides:
  1x4s: (22) 15''
F — Casters:
  (4) 2'' casters and screws
G — Nails:
  1 lb. 4d (1-½'');
  ½-1b 8d (2-½ '')
  finishing nails
H — Yellow glue

FIVE EASY STEPS

Fig. 5

1. Assemble bottom frame (A) with 8d nails and glue.

Fig. 6

2. Glue/nail the four 2x2 corner posts (B) to outside corners of two 1x4 bottom boards (C). Glue/nail the five bottom boards to frame with 4d nails, positioning boards with posts along outside edges.

Fig. 7

3. Glue/nail top frame (D) to corner posts 1-½ below top of post, using 8d nails.

4. Apply 1x4 sides (E) with glue and 4d nails.

5. Attach casters to bottom corners making sure widest part of caster doesn't extend beyond outer edge of box.

Fig. 5

16½"

17½"

Fig. 6

17½"

16½"

Fig. 7

15"

D

E

B

C

A

Table Top

24"x 28-½"

Fig. 8

MATERIALS LIST

A — Table top: 1x12s: (2) 27"
B — Cross brace: 1x2s: (2) 22-½"
C — Edge trim: 1x2s: (4) 30"
D — Nails: ½-lb. 3d (1-¼")
      finishing nails
E — Yellow glue

Fig. 9

1. Assemble 1x12s (A) for
table top by spacing 1x2
cross braces (B) 21-¼ inches
apart and equidistant from each
end. Glue/nail in place, using
3d nails.

2. Cut to size and glue/nail 1x2
trim (C) vertically to table edges.

Fig. 9

B

C

24"

21¼"

28½"

Pull-out Shelves/ Clothes Storage

36"wide x 22-½" deep x 61-½" high, plus casters

MATERIALS LIST

A — Sides: 1x12s: (4) 60"
B — Shelf supports:
      2x2s: (8) 22"
      Nailing cleats (for clothes
      storage): 2x2s: (6) 22"
C — Top and bottom:
      1x12s: (4) 36"
D — Shelves:
      1x12s: (8) 34-½"
E — Back: 1x4s:
      (17) 36"; or ¼" plywood,
      waferwood or hardboard,
      36"x61-½"
F — For clothes storage
      option: Clothes rod and
      brackets
G — Casters: (4) 2-½" or 3"
      casters and screws
H — Nails: ½-lb. 4d (1-½");
      ½-lb. 6d (2")
I — Yellow Glue

CONSTRUCTION STEPS

1. **For Shelf Unit:** To assemble
sides (A), glue/nail shelf supports
(B) across 2x12s at desired spacing.

For Clothes Storage:
Glue/nail 2x2 nailing cleats
across 2x12s at top, bottom and
center of sides (Fig. 13). A shelf
may also be added across top.

2. Glue/nail top and bottom
boards (C) to sides.

3. Install 1x12 shelf boards (D)
with nails.

4. Place unit face down on floor.
To make sure it's square,
measure opposite diagonal corners or use a large framing
square. Apply 1x4s to back
horizontally. Or use solid
backing.

For clothes storage, install
brackets and clothes rod at
desired height.

5. Apply casters at bottom corners of unit.

Fig. 13

Fig. 12

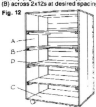

A
B
D

C

Drawers

23-½"wide x 30" long x 4-¼" deep

MATERIALS LIST

A — Drawer front and back:
      1x6: (2) 22"
B — Drawer sides:
      1x6: (2) 30"
C — Bottom supports:
      1x1 (molding stock):
      (2) 22" (front and back)
      (2) 27" (sides)
D — Drawer bottom:
      ¼" plywood, waferboard
      or hardboard: 22"x28-½"
E — Drawer glides: 2x2: (2) 30"
F — Nails: ½-lb. 3d(1-¼");
      ½-lb. 6d (2"); ½-lb. 8d
      (2½")
G — Yellow glue

FOUR SIMPLE STEPS

Fig.10

1. Using a saber saw with fine
tooth blade, cut 6-inch wide by
2-inch deep hand hole in center
of drawer front(A).

2. Glue/nail sides (B) to front and
back with 6d nails.

3. Glue/nail 1x1 drawer bottom
supports (C) to inside of back,
front and sides with 3d nails.
Position supports ¼ inch from
bottom edges. Check to be
certain it's square, then glue/nail
drawer bottom (D) in place.

Fig. 11

4. Position 2x2 drawer glides (E)
1 inch inside front edge of
dividers. Glue/nail in place using
8d (2½") nails.

To install additional drawers,
apply drawer glides 7-½ inches
apart on center. A light coating of
paste wax or candle wax on bottom of drawer sides will help unit
slide easily on glides.

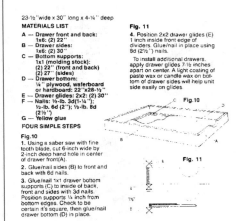

C   **Fig.10**

B

A

Fig. 11

7⅝"

Understair Work Center

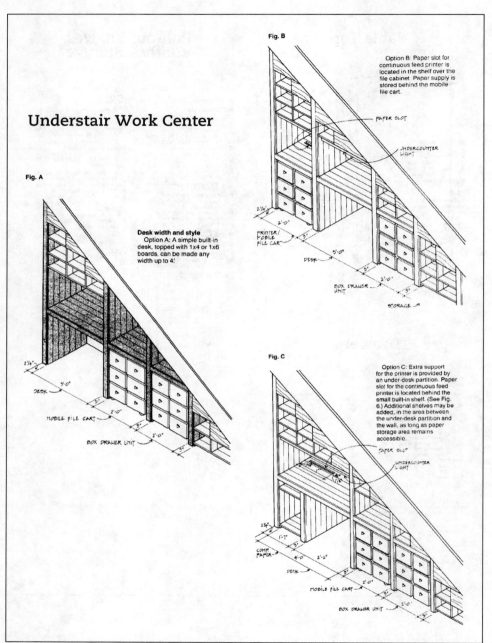

Fig. A

Desk width and style
Option A: A simple built-in desk, topped with 1x4 or 1x6 boards, can be made any width up to 4!

DESK

MOBILE FILE CART

BOX DRAWER UNIT

Fig. B

Option B: Paper slot for continuous feed printer is located in the shelf over the file cabinet. Paper supply is stored behind the mobile file cart.

PAPER SLOT

UNDERCOUNTER LIGHT

PRINTER/ MOBILE FILE CART

DESK

BOX DRAWER UNIT

STORAGE

Fig. C

Option C: Extra support for the printer is provided by an under-desk partition. Paper slot for the continuous feed printer is located behind the small built-in shelf. (See Fig. 6.) Additional shelves may be added, in the area between the under-desk partition and the wall, as long as paper storage area remains accessible.

PAPER SLOT

UNDERCOUNTER LIGHT

COMP PAPER

DESK

MOBILE FILE CART

BOX DRAWER UNIT

Bedrooms & bathrooms

STORAGE requirements for bedrooms vary with the ages and interests of their occupants. Adults generally need ample space for clothing, teens require desks and bookcases, and younger children usually have an abundance of toys and other goodies to be stored.

Most bathrooms are equipped with mirrored cabinets and towel racks. Extra storage is often obtained by adding a vanity, larger cabinet, or shelf unit.

Storage components for both bedrooms and bathrooms should offer a sense of style, as opposed to the plain and simple designs more suited for garages and utility rooms. New storage units in these rooms can be made more attractive simply by including trim or molding and adding stain or paint.

Open, adjustable shelf units serve bedrooms well. Since many family members like to rearrange their bedroom layouts every once in a while, they appreciate being able to adjust shelves to accommodate different items. For permanent storage, a single shelf supported by brackets positioned a foot or so from a bedroom ceiling along one or more walls offers an ideal setting for trophies, doll collections, model cars, and the like.

Bedroom bookcases are another good source of storage. They can hold containers of toys, pictures, stuffed animals, and many other items.

Younger children who like to spend time in their bedrooms playing with toys should relish a system of cabinets and storage boxes made just for them. Such an organizer would also please Mom and Dad, especially when all of the toys are neatly put away at the end of the day. (See illustration at top of next page.)

Bedroom storage options

A wall-to-wall bookcase might just be the thing for schoolwork storage to organize the books, binders, papers, pens and pencils. The bookcase is low and out of the way, but is still easy to reach.

Perfect for the kids' room, the bookcase works especially well along walls with low windows. Select your site making sure the bookcase will not interfere with electrical outlets or doorways.

A 1x12 board is most commonly used for shelving material, although other widths may be used to suit your needs.

Cut the boards to the appropriate length. Remember to subtract the thickness of the end pieces from your measurements. The height of the unit depends on your projected use. However, 12 to 14 inches of space between shelves should accommodate most books.

For a more professional look, attach parallel 1x4s to the underside of the bookcase, lengthwise along the edge. These will act as a footing for the unit.

Use wood screws and metal angle brackets to fasten them. Install vertical dividers between the shelves for added stability and visual appeal. However, the dividers should be no more than 32 inches apart to ensure the proper support.

Also, you may use additional boards to serve as a backing, which will help keep the bookcase square. For added stability, nail the bookcase at either end to wall studs.

As an extra touch, leave four inches of space above the last shelf. Top the unit with a smaller width board, such as a 1x6.

Fill all nail holes with wood putty and sand the unit to a smooth finish. Paint or stain the bookcase to match the room decor, or brush with a clear finish.

Materials Needed: (for a 10-foot long bookcase) 3 pcs. 1x12 in. x 10 ft.; 1 pc. 1x12 in. x 8 ft.; 1 pc. 1x6 in. x 10 ft.; 2 pcs. 1x4 in. x 10 ft.; 1 1/2 in. No. 10 wood screws.

Courtesy of Western Wood Products Association.

Plans for these Kid-Size Storage Modules are available from the WWPA. Ask for Plan Sheet #62. (See illustration at top of next page.)

Under-bed storage

People have been storing things in vacant spaces under beds forever. Problems arise when it comes time to retrieve them. An organized method of better utilizing the space under beds for storage is provided by containers on wheels. (See illustration at bottom of next page.)

Courtesy of Western Wood Products Association.

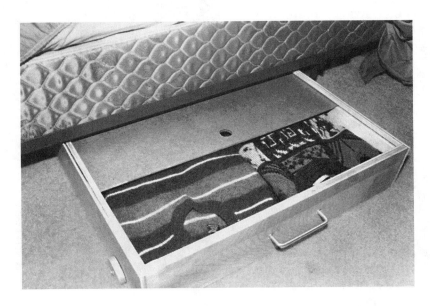

Bedrooms & bathrooms   79

Before building under-bed wheeled containers, take plenty of time to accurately measure and inspect the under-bed space. Some beds sit low to the floor and have center supports that might hinder a container's maneuverability. Account for wheel clearance under the units, too.

Bunk beds generally sit high off floors and provide room for deep containers. Three modules, each about 2 feet wide, can hold lots of toys, clothes, blankets, and so on. For double beds, consider two or three short units on each side.

Three-quarter-inch birch plywood was used for the front, back, and sides of this under-bed module. The bottom and lid are ¼-inch hardboard and the wheels were cut from a piece of 1-x-4 Douglas fir. A ¼-inch straight router bit was employed to cut a groove for the hardboard bottom to ensure a tight fit. The groove for the lid was cut with a ⅜-inch straight bit, allowing extra room for the lid to slide easily back and forth.

Had the groove for the lid been cut more narrow than ⅜ inch, the lid would be difficult to slide back and forth. The lid's bottom edges were sanded smooth to further facilitate its maneuvering.

Although home-improvement centers, hardware stores, and craft outlets generally offer a wide variety of wood and

plastic wheels, you can quickly make your own with a *hole saw*. For best results, use a drill press rather than a hand-held power drill. Attach wheels with wood screws that feature a plain, unthreaded shank near their heads. These shank sections serve as wheel axles. Do not overtighten screws. Bring them up close to wheels but allow enough play for the wheels to rotate.

You can make a simple finger pull on the modules by drilling a small hole in their face. If desired, you can install a handle instead. Use a tape measure to locate the center on the front face, then mark the locations for handle ends. Drill holes through the front face at those points and insert screws into the handles from the inside.

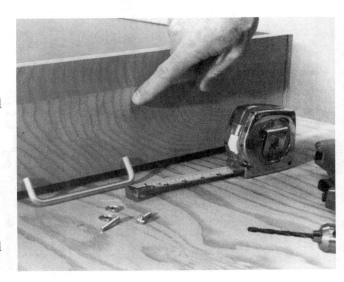

If your family could use an extra bed from time to time, consider a trundle bed. This one consists of a sheet of ¾-inch plywood for the base and front, ⅜-inch plywood for angled supports, and four 2-inch casters underneath. The

mattress is an inexpensive bunk-bed model that is slightly smaller and thinner than regular twin-bed mattresses.

Use fixed casters on a trundle bed. The bed can be moved in and out easier than if you use swivel casters. (See illustration at bottom of page.)

After a good night's sleep, the trundle bed can be rolled conveniently out of the way. (See illustration at top of next page.)

Typical clothes-closet designs do not always utilize all available storage space. Single shelves above hanger rods can be complemented with another, narrower shelf above them. Space under hanging clothes, which is often wasted, can be put to good use with the installation of an open shelf unit.

Organizing closets

One of the better ways to maximize bedroom closet storage is with a Steel Plank Closet Organizer from Stanley. This unit is very easy to install. Although you could complete its installation in just a couple of hours, you might want to plan to spend a day at it to give you time to clean and paint the closet beforehand.

This unit features a shelf across the top that is hidden behind part of the upper wall. Drawers are excellent Closet Organizer options. In addition to helping organize closets, installing these systems offers do-it-yourself homeowners an excellent opportunity to sift through and thin out lots of things from closets that are no longer needed or wanted.

Before the Closet Organizer can be installed, remove existing closet shelves, supports, and rods. Rods generally rest in supports and simply pull out, while boards and metal brackets are nailed or screwed to studs.

Avoid punching holes in drywall by employing a piece of wood behind hammers and pry bars. Without a wood buffer, hammer heads and pry bars can quickly compress drywall, creating dents or holes. Wear safety goggles and avoid wearing any finger or wrist jewelry while engaged in such demolition activities.

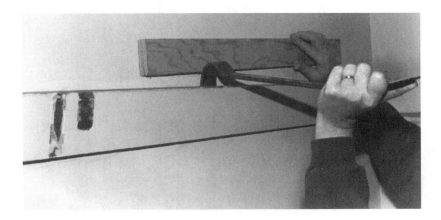

The instructions provided with Stanley's Closet Organizer are very clear, concise, and easy to follow. It might be easiest for you to spread out all parts first to become familiar with them and how they are designed to fit together. Everything you need for installation is enclosed with the system, including drywall anchors and screws for the wall supports, which are seen here with the small mount on the wall in the center of the photo.

Supports slip into the anchors, and vertical tower supports screw into bracket front ends. A support mounted on the right-hand wall is also secured with drywall anchors and screws. Like all of the other wall anchors, its position is easily determined by utilizing the coded holes on the vertical tower supports. (A tower support is used as an anchor-positioning guide before it is installed.) (See illustration at top of next page.)

Looking from floor level, this system provides a long upper shelf with another one on the right designed for tall objects. This Closet Organizer was incredibly quick and easy to install.

Janna is snapping on end caps to the ends of steel planks. Planks snapped onto the tower section are a standard length. Those used for the upper shelves might have to be cut depending upon the width of your closet. To assist you in cutting plank pieces cleanly and evenly, Stanley includes a 32-tooth hacksaw blade in its Closet Organizer packages.

To finish off our project, Janna snaps on covers to the vertical tower supports. These parts cover the supports' open center sections where screws were inserted into brackets. (See illustration at bottom of page.)

In addition to a basic Closet Organizer, these optional drawers offer additional storage space. They are deep and sturdy. Drawer assembly and installation is very easy. In fact, these were the simplest and quickest drawers I have ever put together and installed. It took less than fifteen minutes to assemble, adjust, and secure all three drawers. (See illustrations at top of next page.)

Bathroom storage options

In chapter 8 I discuss in detail on how to build a cabinet with drawers, doors, counter, and sink. That information applies to sink vanities as well, which are assembled in the same manner.

Along with vanities, bathrooms are well served with large mirrored cabinets, towel racks, shelf units, and hooks. In showers and bathtubs, consider waterproof caddies designed to hang from shower heads or fit into corners. Bathrooms with open space might be perfect candidates for bench units complete with hooks above for towels and clothes.

Attractive hooks in many styles are available in home-improvement centers. Instead of simply mounting them directly to walls, enhance their overall appearance with a hardwood backing plate. A router bit created this decorative edge on a piece of leftover oak. It is mounted to the wall with wood screws because there is a stud behind it. Otherwise, drywall anchors would have been used. The hook was then attached to the wood block with its own small wood screws.

If many family members use the same bathroom, you may need additional places to hang towels. The person who designed this towel rack deserves a standing ovation. The four-bar towel rack hangs behind a bathroom door and is supported on the door's hinges.

The behind-the-door towel rack was constructed with a 1¼-inch hardwood dowel for the vertical support, ¾-inch hardwood dowels for the towel hangers, four round hardwood knobs, and two 2½-inch brass corner braces. One side of each corner bracket was cut to about 1½ inches long with a screw hole enlarged to allow the door hinge pins to fit through.

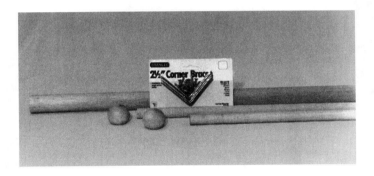

Drilling accurate holes in dowels must be done on a drill press with the dowels secured inside a groove cut into a 2×4 or other board. Be certain that the dowels are solidly clamped in place before drilling.

Many stores and do-it-yourself centers offer various types of attractive towel racks. If so inclined, study models on display and then build your own out of oak or other exotic wood. Be sure to seal and stain them to avoid problems associated with moisture absorption. In addition, mount towel racks securely to walls. If located between studs, use heavy-duty wall anchors rather than small plastic ones.

Kitchens

KITCHEN STORAGE designs are a matter of taste. Some families prefer to have almost everything concealed in cupboards, cabinets, drawers, and pantries. Others like to display pots and pans, wine racks, and dinnerware on hangers or open shelves. With the realization that many homeowners look forward to remodeling existing kitchens, home-improvement centers have established kitchen remodeling departments in their stores. In addition, they have spent a lot of time and money setting up displays of kitchen designs for viewing.

When you begin searching for design ideas, visit these displays. Also, look through home-oriented magazines for new ideas on efficient, convenient, and attractive kitchen storage.

As with storage projects for other household rooms, the Western Wood Products Association offers a number of inexpensive building plans for the kitchen. Some are geared toward novice woodworkers, while others are intended for those with more advanced skills. (See illustration at top of next page.)

Do-it-yourself building plans

The WWPA offers more than one set of plans for kitchen islands. While serving as an additional work counter, kitchen islands provide storage space for pots and pans, cooking utensils, towels, and more. If your kitchen is over a crawl space or basement, it might be easy to equip a new kitchen island with a sink and running water. (See illustration at top left of page 93.)

The kitchen behind this built-in hutch in the dining room was completely stripped down to bare studs and remodeled. The installation of an angled stove/oven cooking center created room for this custom hutch. A picture, mirror, or set of matching shelves can fill this space nicely. (See illustration at top right on page 93.)

Kitchen-storage units

Long used in midwestern country kitchens, the versatile plate shelf is still seen in many of today's modern homes. The shelf can be made from a six-foot 1x10 (actual size 3/4 by 9 1/4 inches) and a eight-foot 1x8 (actual size 3/4 by 7 1/4 inches).

Cut the 1x10, which will be used for the top piece, to your desired shelf length. Three to four feet is usually sufficient. To display plates, use a power saw and guide to cut a 1/4 inch-deep plate groove 2 1/2 inches from the back edge of the top piece. Or, you can attach a piece of half-round moulding the length of the shelf, 2 1/2 inches from the back edge.

For the back piece, cut the 1x8 to the same length as the 1x10, minus 3 1/2 inches. This will allow for the addition of the end supports, plus 1 inch of overlap of the top piece on either end.

Cut the middle and end supports from the remainder of the 1x8. The end pieces should be 6 1/2 by 7 inches, with the middle support at 6 1/2 by 5 3/4 inches.

Next, make a template for the supports from a pattern of your choice. Trace the template onto the support pieces, then use a jigsaw to cut the patterns out.

(Note: Be sure that the wood grain runs horizontally in the supports). Use wood glue and 2-inch-long No. 8 screws to attach the middle and end supports to the backing. Be sure to countersink all screw holes.

Mount the top piece using No. 8 screws, allowing for a one-inch overhang on the end supports.

For a finished look, apply half-round moulding to the front and side edges of the shelf and cove mouldings applied underneath the lip of the shelf. Use a nail set and 1 1/4 inch finishing nails to apply the mouldings. Fill the nail holes with wood putty. Optional wood pegs or brass hooks can be attached to the face of the shelf. Sand the shelf being sure to smooth any rough or sharp edges. Then apply a wood oil or transparent finish. Install the shelf on a wall using No. 10, 2 1/4 inch-long screws through the back piece. Make sure to screw into the solid wood of wall studs.

Materials Needed: 1 pc. 1x10 in. x 6 ft.; 1 pc. 1x8 in. x 10 ft.; 2 pcs. moulding 3/4 in. x 44 in.; 2 in. No. 8 wood screws; 2 1/4 in. No. 10 wood screws; 1 1/4 in. finishing nails.

Courtesy of Western Wood Products Association.

Kitchen pantries are ideal accessories for kitchen storage. They normally offer room to store food, small appliances, and other necessities. One of the more common complaints about pantries, however, is that they aren't well-organized. Too often, items get lost or overlooked when shoved behind taller things, especially on the lowest and highest shelves. (See illustration at bottom margin on next page.)

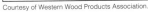
Courtesy of Western Wood Products Association.

Sets of heavy-duty drawers are ideal for lower pantry storage convenience. If desired, the entire bottom compartment can be filled with drawers that slide out to offer full views of and easy access to their contents. Adjustable storage shelves above accommodate storage for items of various heights. (See illustration at top left of next page.)

Use heavy-duty guides for pantry drawers because they should be expected to be able to support a good amount of weight. As seen here, drawer guides are secured to pieces of wood that fill spaces between pantry side panels and inner edges of side stile trim pieces. If the sides of your pantry are exposed and consist of panels less than ¾ inch thick, consider lining the interiors with ¾-inch plywood glued to side panels. Drawer-guide support boards can then be screwed to the plywood, eliminating the need to insert screws through the exposed side of thin-walled pantries. (See illustration at top right of next page.)

Kitchens 93

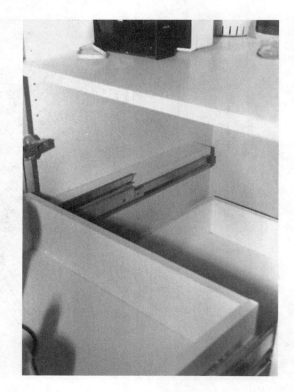

Notice that these pantry drawers are rather shallow. They were built this way to offer maximum visibility of their contents. In addition, the extra space above the bottom drawer allows plenty of room for tall objects, such as blenders and juice makers.

Corner storage

Too often, corner cabinets don't get used because access to them is so difficult. Storage space is certainly plentiful but how does one easily retrieve things tucked way back into those corner spaces?

Perhaps a lazy Susan is the answer? Without its revolving trays, this corner cabinet unit would be almost useless. Cabinet doors are secured together with trays attached to them, making this a complete and sturdy storage accessory. Lazy-Susan kits and similar accessories are available at home-improvement centers, kitchen-and-bath remodeling outlets, and cabinet-supply houses.

Special mounts are located at the top and bottom of the cabinet. They must be located and installed accurately. Be certain to follow directions carefully.

Attach the cabinet-door panels to pieces of plywood to form a complete door unit. Plywood serves as solid support for trays and mounting hardware. Pencil lines on the back sides of the plywood denote exact locations for tray attachments. (See illustration at top of next page.)

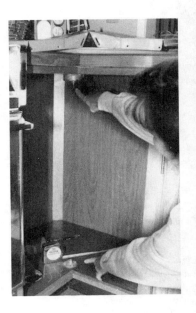

An adjustable roller and indent mechanism on this top mounting unit serves as a door stop. When the door unit approaches the closed position, the roller slips into an indentation to hold the door closed.

Backing pieces of ¾-inch hardwood plywood are secured together at a right angle with wood glue and screws. The screws on the back sides secure front panel doors that match other kitchen cabinet and cupboard doors. (See illustration at top of next page.)

In order for the revolving doors to rotate freely past adjacent trim, the outer edges must be *chamfered*; that is, cut at an angle. If they were left square, they would hit the trim on each pass. In addition, since the chamfer edge was cut deep toward the back of the doors, full-size front edge corners near the trim make the unit appear as if it consists of just two small doors.

Different brands and styles of lazy-Susan units require different installation techniques and methods. Since cabinet fit and finish are such important factors for this type of accessory, you might want to consult an experienced cabinetmaker before starting such a project. Special installation instructions and handy tips from someone who has installed many similar units might help you complete your project with minimal problems and better results.

Organizing kitchen utensils

Most of us keep spoons, forks, and knives separated in handy, plastic drawer organizers. But what about large cutting knives? Often they are scattered in different drawers.

Since most knives are made of metal, a magnetic bar works great for holding them next to a cutting board or a food-preparation area. Simple units like this are commonly available. They are mounted to walls with screws or anchors.

Does your kitchen knife drawer look like this? Not only is this inconvenient, it is also a hazard. Reaching into a drawer full of sharp knives is just asking for cut fingers or hands. With just three small pieces of wood, you can change a drawer like this into an organized and safe knife-storage compartment.

This piece of oak received a number of shallow cuts on a table saw. Saw kerfs extend through ¾ of the wood's thickness, and they are spaced about ¾ inch apart. The extra-wide kerf was made with two passes on the table saw. It can support double blades for an electric knife. (See illustration at left.)

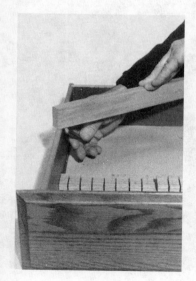

To serve as a guard against pointed knife ends and to provide a separate compartment in this drawer, a second board can be cut to fit diagonally across the drawer. Place all of the knives in the drawer to determine the best location for the board. Then

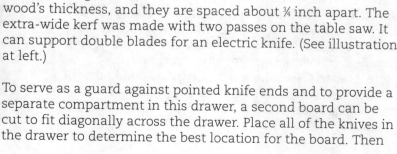

rest the board on top of the drawer in its intended position and carefully mark the angle for cutting.

With both boards in place, make light pencil marks on the drawer bottom to serve as hole-drilling guides. Drill two holes for each board, then insert screws through the bottom.

This drawer is much nicer to look at, safer, and offers much more convenience than before. A ¼-inch-thick slat was secured with double back tape to the drawer bottom next to the front. It holds knife handles up slightly, preventing the sharp ends from sticking up. (See illustrations at top and bottom of next page.)

Just about every kitchen drawer can be made to store things more conveniently with the addition of partitions. If you desire, make a series of wood trays with dividers that could be stacked on top of each other for maximum storage. Tray depths might vary to accommodate larger items. The top tray could have a handle to make it easy to remove.

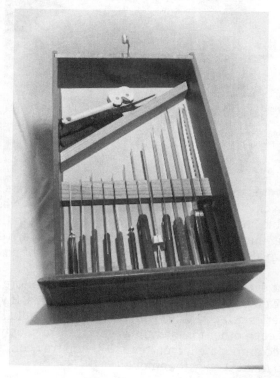

100   Home Storage

Recycling cans, newspapers, and other household items has become an important and common concern. Many homeowners are now required to separate various items into segregated containers for pickup. This has created yet another household-storage concern. Building a recycling center like this one might prove to be a useful and convenient project. (See illustrations through to page 106.)

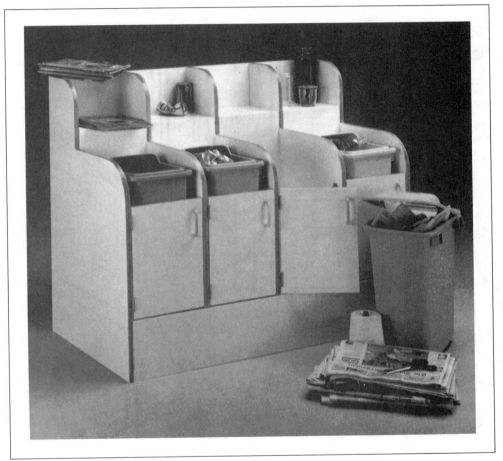

Courtesy of American Plywood Association.

MATERIALS LIST - Recycling Center

Recommended Panels:

Quantity	Description
3	APA trademarked Medium Density Overlay (MDO) panels, overlaid both sides. Other types of APA panels may be substituted. Size 3/4 in. × 4 ft. × 8 ft.

Other Materials:

Quantity	Description
As required	1×1 lumber cleats
As required	1-1/2 in. #8 flathead wood screws
As required	Construction glue
8	3/4 × 2 in. hinges
4	Magnetic door catches
4	Door pulls
As required	Paint or stain

Project Notes:

Begin by building the platform base. Cut the bottom to fit inside the two 8 × 46-1/4-inch plywood rails. With the base completed, cut the back piece and two end panels and attach them to the base. The upper platform is composed of four, 23-3/4 × 11-inch sections fastened to cleats. Leave a 3/4-inch space between the sections so dividers can be inserted. After dropping the dividers in place, attach the doors to the dividers and end pieces with hinges. Install a magnetic catch behind each door. For portability, the unit can be mounted on casters.

Finishing

Finish the recycling center with two coats of polyurethane varnish or paint if the project is made with overlaid panels. A stain can be used on other types of panels. A face primer is recommended prior to applying top-coat finish.

Designer: Stephen Mead

Snap-'N Cycle Bins provided by Rubbermaid.

Panel Layout

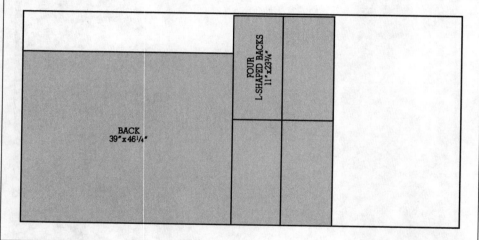

BACK
39" x 46¼"

FOUR
L-SHAPED BACKS
11" x 23¾"

Courtesy of American Plywood Association.

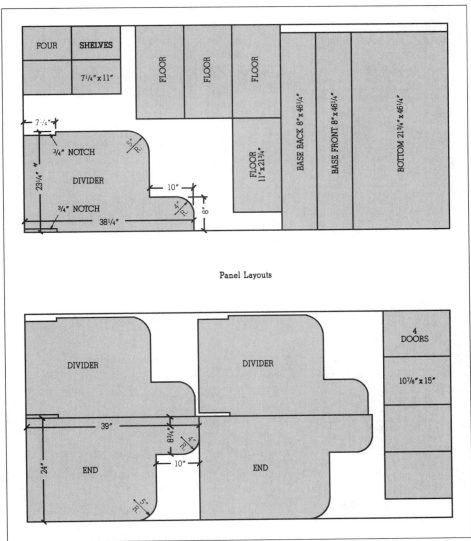

FOUR | SHELVES

7¼" x 11"

FLOOR

FLOOR

FLOOR

FLOOR 11" x 21¼"

BASE BACK 8" x 46¼"

BASE FRONT 8" x 46¼"

BOTTOM 21¾" x 46¼"

7¼"

¾" NOTCH

5° R.

23¼"

DIVIDER

10"

¾" NOTCH

4" R.

8"

38¼"

Panel Layouts

DIVIDER

DIVIDER

4 DOORS

10⅞" x 15"

39"

8¾"

4" R.

10"

24"

END

END

5° R.

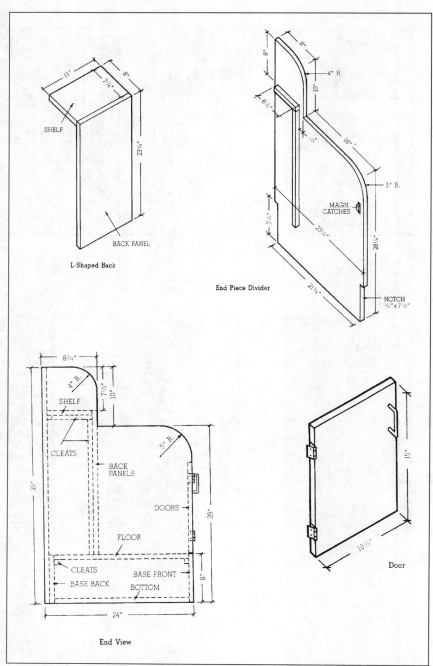

SHELF

BACK PANEL

L-Shaped Back

End Piece Divider

4" R.

MAGN.
CATCHES

NOTCH
¾" x 7¼"

SHELF

CLEATS

BACK
PANELS

DOORS

FLOOR

CLEATS

BASE BACK

BASE FRONT

BOTTOM

End View

Door

104   Home Storage

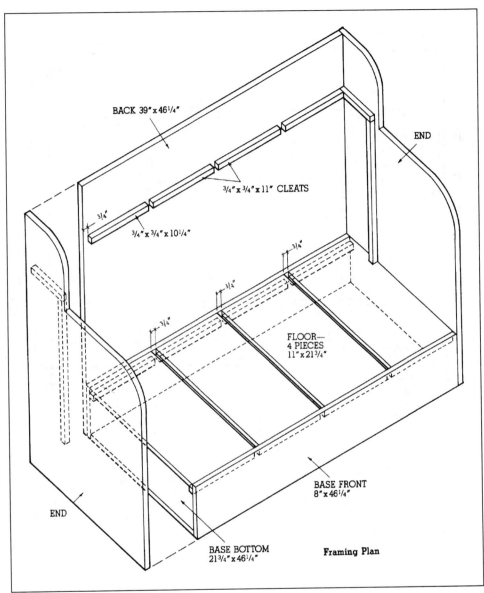

BACK 39" x 46¼"

¾" x ¾" x 11" CLEATS

END

¾"

¾" x ¾" x 10¼"

¾"

¾"

¾"

FLOOR—
4 PIECES
11" x 21¾"

BASE FRONT
8" x 46¼"

END

BASE BOTTOM
21¾" x 46¼"

Framing Plan

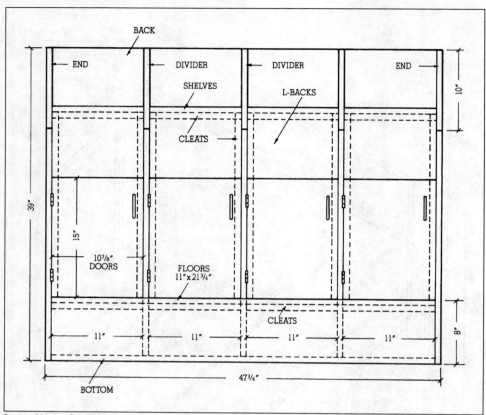

BACK

END   DIVIDER   DIVIDER   END

                        SHELVES

                                          L-BACKS

                   CLEATS

10"

39"

15"

10⁷⁄₈"
DOORS

FLOORS
11" x 21³⁄₄"

CLEATS

8"

11"   11"   11"   11"

47³⁄₄"

BOTTOM

Sinks, counters, & cabinets

WHETHER THEY function as vanities, kitchen counters, or utility sinks, wide cabinets outfitted with shelves, drawers, a work top, and a sink provide versatile home storage accessories. With a little time spent inspecting cabinet and counter displays in stores and in homes, you can design your own model. If you prefer, send for catalogs of plans from the Western Wood Products Association, the American Plywood Association, and any of a number of companies that offer plans for sale through ads in do-it-yourself magazines.

Like other home-storage units, quality is based upon the materials and hardware that are used in their construction. The degree of craftsmanship also plays a major role. Learning how to design and create intricate cabinet and fine woodworking pieces requires a great deal of practice and study. With that in mind, this chapter demonstrates how to build an efficient, sturdy, and yet modest unit using plywood and fir.

Cabinet and counter dimensions are very important. Units must be able to fit in spaces selected for them, the height should be accommodating, and the depth should be functional without causing interference.

Cabinets and counters can be as long as desired. Available space generally dictates this dimension. Most counters are around 34 to 36 inches tall, but this dimension can be altered to suit your family's personal preference. Many work counters are around 26 inches deep, with some bathroom models measuring 22 to 24 inches, depending on bathroom size and sink style. To help you determine dimensions that best fit your needs and physical size, measure kitchen, bathroom, and other counters in your home to see which dimensions feel most ideal.

Assembling basic cabinets

This sink, counter, and cabinet unit was custom built to fit in a prescribed space. It could be installed in a workshop bathroom or a darkroom. The sink is located slightly off center to offer a small counter area on the left and a bigger work surface to the right. Cabinet doors are centered under the sink, with three narrow drawers on the left and three large drawers on the right. The prefabricated 5-foot-long-×-2-foot-deep countertop was purchased at a home-improvement center for about $20.

Regular ¾-inch A/C plywood is used for the base and interior panels and ¾-inch birch plywood for outside panels. With the front side on the floor, a finish nailer is used to secure a side panel to the base. Notice the light pencil line on the side panel, which serves as a nailing guide. The base fits into a ¾-inch groove on the inside of the side panel that was cut with a router. (See margin illustration on next page.)

A 3⅝-inch-high-×-3-inch-deep notch was cut in the front bottom corner of the side panel to serve as a *toekick*, or *kickspace*; that is, an open space for feet. The dimension was designated in the instructions for a NuTone kickspace heater that will be installed under the unit later. Regular toekick or kickspace dimensions range from 3 to 4 inches in both directions.

Here, the cabinet is upright. A piece of plywood running horizontally on the right serves as the top rear cabinet support rail. One-quarter-inch hardboard has been nailed to the base, side panels, and rail to serve as a back and to help keep the entire unit square.

Triangular wood blocks serve as braces to reinforce cabinet corners. They are glued and screwed in place. Screw heads on this panel are not visible as this side of the unit is against a wall.

Triangular blocks should be installed at every right angle along countertops. After spreading glue on the mating surfaces, use Quick-Grip clamps to hold them together. Carefully drive screws through the wood piece and into the cabinet side panel to avoid visible screw heads. Drill pilot holes for all screws to prevent wood from cracking. (See illustration at top of next page.)

While building a cabinet or counter unit, it is easiest to rotate the project upside down and from side to side to make it more accessible. With the unit now on its top, a 2-x-4 runner is secured at the kickspace. Another 2-x-4 runner is located at the back of the unit.

The 2×4s support the bulk of the unit's weight. Without them, side panels would have to bear all the weight. Nails are driven through side panels and down from the top of the base.

Dimension lumber, such as 2×4s, is not always milled as perfectly as finished materials. If need be, use a *block plane* to smooth the bows and imperfections in 2-x-4 runners.

Basic cabinet and counter construction is similar to other shelf and cabinet accessories, with two side panels, a base, and a top. The dimensions are different and so is the kickspace. Take your time building units like this to ensure corners remain square. Use a router with a ¾-inch straight bit to make grooves for the panels.

Rails are trim pieces that run horizontally on a cabinet. Their vertical counterparts are called *stiles*. These rails and stiles were glued and then further secured with finishing nails. A lot of time was spent with tape measure, pencil, and paper trying to come up with a suitable design for the placement and dimensions of the doors and drawers. This also entailed

Installing front trim

measuring the different items that will be kept in the unit, which is why a big, deep drawer was included at bottom right. A single, long rail extends from the left side of the unit to the right to provide added horizontal support for all of the panels.

Plywood panels separate the under-sink door area from both left- and right-drawer sections. This adds support for the top, and it provides a means to connect small shelves on the inside of the door space.

The rails and stiles were made from 1-x-2 Douglas fir. The fir was bought with rounded corners, which is a typical milling operation. But rounded corners are not suitable for rails and stiles. Therefore, each board was run through the *jointer* to create straight, square edges.

Notice how square this stile is after being run through the jointer. The notch for the stile was cut using a *trim saw* set to the proper depth. First make a series of passes with the saw to leave thin slats of wood in the notch area. Then use a sharp chisel to clean out the notch. The stile is glued and nailed into the notch.

Joints where rails and stiles meet must be filled with wood dough or putty and then sanded smooth. If you carefully follow instructions on the label, your efforts should result in near invisible joints.

Sanding is made easier with power tools. Do not expect quick sanding jobs to offer great results. Quality sanding takes time and patience. It is the last step before applying sealer and stain or paint. Extra time spent sanding to perfection rewards you with an excellent stain or paint finish, while stain or paint will tend to highlight the flaws in a mediocre sanding job. (See illustration at top of next page.)

Making drawers

Drawer dimensions are regulated by the size of rail and stile openings, depth of counter units, and specifications in drawer-guide hardware instructions. Most drawer guides require about ½-inch clearance on each side. Failure to account for drawer-guide hardware dimensions can result in drawers that wobble or fit too tight.

Drawers are commonly made with ½-inch A/C plywood for the back, sides, and front, with a hardboard bottom. You can opt for other materials as you see fit. To ensure extra support for heavy objects placed in them, drawers for the bathroom/darkroom counter were made with ¾-inch A/C plywood for the back, sides, and front and ⅜-inch A/C plywood for the bottom.

A router is very useful for drawer construction. Use a straight bit to create grooves for drawer bottoms and a straight bit or rabbet bit to make rabbets on the ends of side panels. Always be certain your work is securely clamped in place before you begin routing. Also, wear safety goggles and a dust mask.

In lieu of a router, grooves for drawer bottoms can be made with a dado attached to your table saw. Test dado cuts on a piece of scrap wood first. Follow all instructions for setting up dado assemblies to ensure safe and efficient work.

Grooves cut along the bases of drawer panels make it a bit tough to figure out exact dimensions for drawer bottoms, as bottom panels must rest inside grooves for support. An easy way to determine this size is by reversing a front or back panel and clamping it between both side panels. This way, you can precisely see and measure the distance from inside the groove on one side panel to the inside of the groove on the other panel to determine the bottom-panel width. (See illustration at top of next page.)

Sandwich the front and back panels together back-to-back and measure the thickness of wood between both grooves. Subtract that measurement from the length of side panels to determine an accurate drawer bottom length.

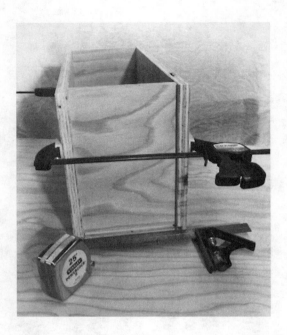

Resting on its side, this deep, narrow drawer's front and back panels have been glued and nailed to a side panel. To the right, the drawer's ⅜-inch plywood bottom has been slipped into place inside the panels' grooves. Drawer bottoms are not generally glued or nailed in place. Rather, they are left free to float.

With drawer-guide hardware, drawers are typically tipped up to be installed and removed. This operation requires maneuvering room, created here by cutting away a portion of the top of the drawer sides. Plan to make drawer panels about ¾ to 1 inch shorter than the actual space between counter rails. Notice the nails on the side of the stile. They will be set, filled with wood dough, and sanded.

Likewise, be sure to follow drawer-guide dimension specifications for drawer width. Guides require a specific opening along drawer sides to fit and function properly. (See illustration at top of next page.)

Different types of drawer guides might specify larger or smaller open space dimensions. Not all guides are the same. The cabinet in the top illustration on page 119 is from a different unit, made with ½-inch plywood and hardboard.

Notice the drawer guide located inside this counter. A piece of 1×2 supports the guide between the front stile and rear counter back. It was needed because the side of the stile extended into the drawer opening by about ¾ inch, much like the kitchen-pantry drawer unit featured earlier. (See illustration at top of next page.)

Another means of providing drawer support is with wood rails or runners. Pieces of 1×2 have been screwed into the counter's ¾-inch plywood side panel and interior plywood panel. The drawer simply slides on top of these boards without the use of guide hardware. An angle drill/driver comes in handy for this type of screw installation. (See illustration at bottom of next page.)

Drawer runners for top drawers serve as stops for lower drawers. As drawers are pulled out, their rear sections tend to move upward as the part pulled out of the counter tends to fall down. Stops for top drawers must be installed as well. Without them, drawers can fall out when they are opened. This is not a problem when you use drawer-guide hardware.

The screws used to secure runners to counter side panels must be long enough to ensure a solid hold onto plywood but not so long as to penetrate through. In some cases, you might have to use shorter screws that require a countersink hole to achieve adequate and secure penetration.

Drawer-guide hardware instructions clearly indicate how guides are designed to be installed so that drawers rest on them straight, level, and even. With wood runners, it might be easiest to screw them in place rather tightly at the front only and then insert drawers. Use a square to determine when drawers are lined up flush, adjusting the runners from below.

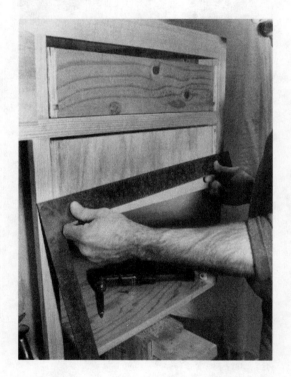

A single screw tightened at the front of a runner should be enough to hold its back end in place with an empty drawer on top of it. Once the drawer has been positioned flush with the front of the counter and the runner adjusted up to the bottom of the drawer, install and tighten screws at the back and middle of the runners.

Plywood features definite wood-grain patterns. If at all possible, try to cut drawer fronts in an order that allows drawers to maintain that pattern. Such a pattern is clearly evident on these three small drawer fronts. This is not important for units that will be painted, but it is a nice touch for those scheduled for stain.

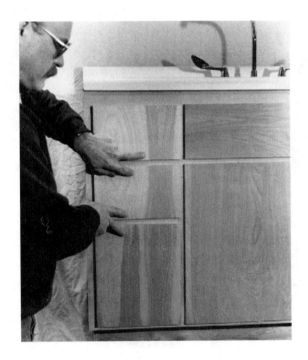

These birch-plywood drawer fronts were not cut in order out of the same section of a plywood sheet. Notice that their wood grains do not match. However, they fit nicely and feature rounded edges made with a shaper and round cutter head. A ⅜-x-⅜-inch rabbet was cut all the way around each drawer front to allow a portion of the fronts to actually go inside the drawer space. This will keep debris from filtering into the drawer spaces.

Drawer fronts are secured to base drawer units with screws inserted from inside. One easy method of aligning drawer fronts with drawers is with clamps. Here, a rabbeted door front is placed in position and the drawer gently brought up to it. With everything aligned, clamps are attached. Pilot holes can then be drilled and screws installed to complete the operation.

As hard as you try, there might be times when rabbeted drawer fronts are positioned too tightly against rails and stiles. For those occasions, a Makita 1⅛-inch *belt sander* works great to sand away small amounts of the drawer-front rabbet to create a perfect fit.

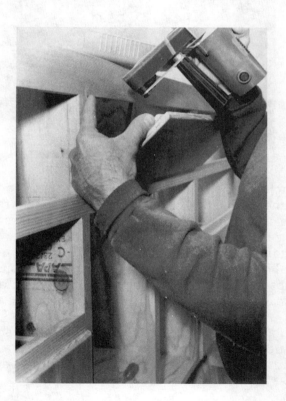

Cabinet and counter doors are easiest to install while the units are flat on their backs. This way, doors can be placed in position and adjusted without falling or tilting from side to side.

Door hinges are generally placed about 2 to 4 inches down from the top and up from the bottom. Attach hinges to doors first and then place doors on cabinet or counter units that have been laid on their back for final placement and installation.

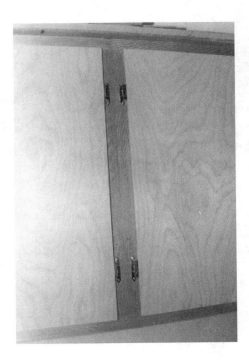

Home-improvement centers carry a wide variety of door hinges in all sorts of styles, colors, and materials. Rabbeted doors require a special hinge. These hinges typically fit ⅜-x-⅜-inch rabbets. Before opting for other door edge rabbet dimensions, be sure that you can buy hinges that will fit properly. (See illustration at top of next page.)

An easy way to start hinge screws straight and in their correct position is with a *screw set*. This tool features a spring-loaded pointed pin shaft located inside a cylindrical body. The body's rounded nose is placed into hinge screw openings and the end of the shaft is tapped with a hammer. (See illustration at top of next page.)

The pointed shaft creates a small pilot hole for screws. Set one screw hole first and insert a screw, then adjust the hinge as necessary before setting and installing the next screw. Install screws one by one to ensure hinges are not inadvertently moved in the process. Do the same for securing hinges to cabinet or counter units.

Cabinets and counters must be secured to walls to ensure solid support and serve as efficient work surfaces. Placed next to a wall, put a level on top and adjust units as

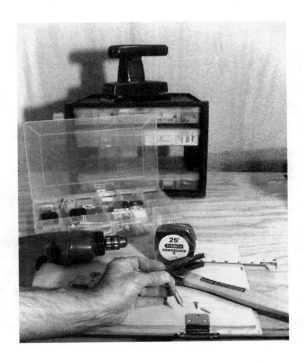

necessary with shims under their 2×4 bottom supports. Once they are leveled, secure units to studs with long wood screws. Run a bead of caulk along the top edge of the backsplash to finish the installation and cover any minor gaps between it and the wall.

Counters equipped with sinks are well served by a handy tray located just in front of them. A tray can hold bars of soap, sponges, rubber gloves, and so on. A few different brands and styles are available utilizing different types of hinges and stops. Although more expensive, units with spring-loaded hinges are most effective and convenient.

Accessorizing counters

Prefabricated countertops are not generally equipped with holes in them for sinks. There is no way for manufacturers to know what size sink any one customer plans to install. Regular countertops are also installed in one piece with no access for sinks. (See illustration at top of next page.)

Cutting sink holes in countertops is easy. The directions for installing this Kohler model were simple, clear, and easy to follow. You'll need a jig saw and a drill to make an entrance hole for the jig saw blade. Directions show you how to secure sinks to counter tops and how to install sink strainers using *plumbers' putty* for a waterproof seal.

Once the sink strainer has been set in plumbers' putty above, additional parts below are screwed on to finish the installation. Sinks typically require 1¼-inch inside diameter

126   **Home Storage**

drain pipes that connect to the household drain pipe with threaded parts and washers. Water is supplied through shutoff valves and flexible tubing. Kits like this one from PlumbShop include all the parts generally required for sink installations.

Notice that holes were cut in the back to allow access for plumbing utilities. Accomplish this task by simply transferring measurements of the pipes sticking out of a wall to the back of your counter, and bore the holes with a hole saw.

The lack of open wall space for a wall heater in the bathroom/darkroom presented a problem that was solved by the installation of a NuTone kickspace heater. This unit can push out warm air at floor level on cold winter days. Instructions are specific with regard to electrical wiring and the open space required for a safe and efficient installation. Kickspace heaters are available in 120- and 240-volt models.

Prefabricated countertops are purchased complete with backsplash components. If you build your own countertop out of ¾-inch plywood and plastic laminate, you'll also have to provide a backsplash. This one was made with sections of 1-x-4 fir. The top edges were rounded with a router and sanded smooth.

Bottom edges were run through a joiner to ensure that they would be perfectly flat and even for installation. They are secured to studs with finishing nails that were set and filled.

Installing cupboards

Spaces occupied by cabinets and counters often provide space above for cupboards. You will need help with their installation, as someone must hold them steady while screws are driven through back support rails and into studs. For safety, place short 2×4s or 2×6s on the counter below and rest cupboards on them in their installation position. If necessary, use thin wood shims to raise the cupboard into position.

This double-door cupboard features a shelf solidly fixed in the middle. You could outfit cupboards with an adjustable shelf system to accommodate storage of various sizes. (See illustration at top of next page.)

These perpendicular cupboards were installed in such a way that an open space exists in the corner. This space might be perfect for storing long rolls of wrapping paper, bolts of sewing fabric, and other tall items. Either cupboard could have been installed into the corner if top and bottom rails and an end stile were eliminated. That cupboard space would be hard to see into and access, but it could serve to store seldom-needed items.

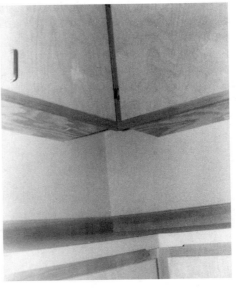

Sinks, counters, & cabinets   129

Overview

Putting together any number of home-storage projects not only provides you and your family with additional and better-organized storage options, it also gives you plenty of practice using different tools and perfecting various woodworking and home-improvement skills. As you continue to advance your skills, you should be able to read and follow more intricate plans for building fine pieces of home-storage furniture made from exotic wood and more expensive materials and hardware.

Since more and more homeowners are choosing to tackle their own home-improvement projects, home-improvement centers and other do-it-yourself outlets have realized that they must hire employees with experience in home construction and woodworking. This assures customers that they can receive intelligent and enlightening answers to questions they have regarding any number of different home-improvement projects. So, don't be afraid to ask questions when purchasing tools or materials.

I hope the information and pictures in this book have helped you learn how different types of home-storage projects are assembled and installed. Remember to follow all of the operating instructions for the tools you use, properly adjust and employ all tool safety guards, wear goggles, dust masks, and hearing protection, and have a safe and enjoyable time with your family while you all work together on your projects.

Sources

THE FOLLOWING companies and organizations supplied information and assistance in this project. I selected them because I am familiar with their quality products and high level of customer service. I recommend that you contact them for additional information and product catalogs.

Alta Industries
P.O. Box 2764
Santa Rosa, CA 95405
(707) 544-5009
(tool belts and pouches)

American Plywood Association
P.O. Box 11700
Tacoma, WA 98411
(206) 565-6600
(information and building plans for plywood)

American Tool Companies, Inc.
P.O. Box 337
De Witt, NE 68341
(402) 683-2315
(Vise-Grip, Quick-Grip, Prosnip, CHESCO, and more tools)

Autodesk Retail Products
11911 North Creek Parkway South
Bothell, WA 98011
(800) 228-3601
(plans-making computer software)

Behr Process Corporation
3400 West Segerstrom Avenue
Santa Ana, CA 92704
(800) 854-0133
(paint, stain, varnish, sealers, and more)

Campbell Hausfeld
100 Production Drive
Harrison, OH 45030
(513) 367-4811
(air compressors, pneumatic tools, and accessories)

Cedar Shake and Shingle Bureau
515 116th Avenue NE, Suite 275
Bellevue, WA 98004-5294
(206) 453-1323
(information regarding cedar shakes and shingles)

DAP, Inc.
P.O. Box 277
Dayton, OH 45401
(800) 568-4554
(sealants, caulking, adhesives, and more)

Eagle Windows and Doors
375 East Ninth Street
Dubuque, IA 52004
(319) 556-2270
(high-quality wood windows and doors)

The Eastwood Company
580 Lancaster Avenue, Box 3014
Malvern, PA 19355-0714
(800) 345-1178
(automotive and metalworking tools and supplies)

Empire Brushes, Inc.
U.S. 13 North
P.O. Box 1606
Greenville, NC 27835-1606
(919) 758-4111
(brushes, brooms, and accessories)

Freud
P.O. Box 7187
High Point, NC 27264
(800) 472-7307
(tools)

General Cable Company (Romex®)
4 Tesseneer Drive
Highland Heights, KY 41076
(606) 572-8000
(electrical wire)

Häfele America Company
3901 Cheyenne Drive
P.O. Box 4000
Archdale, NC 27263
(910) 889-2322
(cabinet and furniture hardware of all types)

Halo Lighting (Cooper Lighting)
400 Busse Road
Elk Grove Village, IL 60007
(708) 956-8400
(recessed ceiling lights)

Harbor Freight Tools (Central Purchasing, Inc.)
3491 Mission Oaks Boulevard
Camarillo, CA 95008
(800) 423-2567
(home-improvement tools, supplies, and more)

Keller Industries, Inc.
18000 State Road Nine
Miami, FL 33162
(800) 222-2600
(ladders, attic stairways, and accessories)

Kohler Company
444 Highland Drive
Kohler, WI 53044
(414) 457-4441
(bathroom fixtures and accessories)

Leslie-Locke, Inc.
4501 Circle 75 Parkway, Suite F-6300
Atlanta, GA 30339
(roof windows, skylights, heat ducting, and more)

Leviton Manufacturing Company, Inc.
59-25 Little Neck Parkway
Little Neck, NY 11362-2591
(718) 229-4040
(electrical switches, receptacles, and more)

Makita USA, Inc.
14930 Northam Street
La Mirada, CA 90638-5753
(714) 522-8088
(power and cordless tools and equipment)

McGuire-Nicholas Company, Inc.
2331 Tubeway Avenue
City of Commerce, CA 90040
(213) 722-6961
(tool belts, pouches, knee pads, back braces, and more)

NuTone
Madison and Red Bank Roads
Cincinnati, OH 45227-1599
(800) 543-8687
(built-in convenience products)

Owens-Corning Fiberglas Insulation
Fiberglas Tower
Toledo, OH 43659
(800) 342-3745
(pink insulation for ceilings, floors, and walls)

PanelLift Telpro, Inc.
Route 1, Box 138
Grand Forks, ND 58201
(800) 441-0551
(drywall lift equipment)

Plano Molding Company
431 East South Street
Plano, IL 60545-1601
(800) 874-6905
(plastic tool boxes, storage units, shelves, and more)

PlumbShop
(a division of Brass Craft)
39600 Orchard Hill Place
Novi, MI 48376
(810) 305-6000
(plumbing supplies)

Power Products Company (SIMKAR)
Cayuga and Ramona Streets
Philadelphia, PA 19120
(800) 346-7833
(fluorescent lighting)

Power Tool Institute, Inc.
1300 Sumner Avenue
Cleveland, OH 44115-2851
(216) 241-7333
(information on safe power-tool operations)

Quality Doors
603 Big Stone Gap
Duncanville, TX 75137
(800) 950-3667
(cabinet doors and refacing materials)

Simpson Strong-Tie Connector Company, Inc.
1450 Doolittle Drive
San Leandro, CA 94577
(800) 999-5099
(metal connectors)

The Stanley Works
1000 Stanley Drive
New Britain, CT 06053
(800) 551-5936
(hand tools, hardware, closet organizers, and more)

Sta-Put Color Pegs
23504 29th Avenue
West Lynnwood, WA 98036-8318
(plastic pegboard hooks)

Structron Corporation
1980 Diamond Street
San Marcos, CA 92069
(619) 744-6371
(garden and construction tools)

Tyvek (DuPont)
Chestnut Run WR-2058
Wilmington, DE 19880-0722
(800) 448-9835
(Housewrap)

U.S. Ceramic Tile Company
P.O. Box 338
East Sparta, OH 44626
(216) 866-5531
(ceramic tile)

Weiser Lock
6660 South Broadmoor Road
Tucson, AZ 85746
(602) 741-6200
(door locks, handles, and knobs)

Western Wood Products Association
522 SW Fifth Avenue
Portland, OR 97204-2122
(503) 224-3930
(information and building plans)

Zircon Corporation
1580 Dell Avenue
Campbell, CA 95008
(408) 866-8600
(water levels and other devices)

sink installation, 107, 125-128, **126**, **127**
stiles, 111-113, **112**, **113**, **114**
supports, 109, **109**
toekick or kickspace, 108-109
trim installation, 111-113, **112**, **113**, **114**
wall-attachment of cabinets, 124-125
cutting guides, 18, **18**

D

dadoes, 33, **33**, 39-40, **40**, 115
DAP Inc., 26, 132
designing storage, 1-11
  attic storage, 10, 45, 51-56
  basement storage, 45, 49-51, **49**, **50**, **51**
  bathroom storage, 88-89, **88**, **89**
  bedroom storage, 77-87
  bookcase, simple design, 3, **3**
  coffee tables as storage, 3
  cupboards and cabinets, 4-5, **4**
  drawers for storage, 8, **8**
  file cabinets as storage, 4
  finding storage ideas:
    magazines, literature, 1-2
  garage storage, 4-5, 46-48, **46**, **47**, **48**
  height considerations for storage spaces, 9
  hooks for storage, 8
  kitchen storage, 91-106
  laundry room storage, 10, 62-63, **62**, **63**
  living-area storage ideas, 2-4
  positioning for easy access, 9
  sewing room storage, 62-63, **62**, **63**
  shelving, 5-8, 5, **6**, **7**
  simple ideas to expand storage, xi-xii

size considerations for storage space, 9
skylights for light and ventilation, 10, **10**
utilities: pipes and wiring behind walls, 9
utility room storage, 10, 62-63, **62**, **63**
video- and audiotape storage, reconditioned icebox, 3, **3**
windows for light and ventilation, 10
Dirt Catcher Pan, 28
doors, hanging counter doors, 123-125, **123**, **124**, **125**
drawer-guide hardware installation, 117-120, **118**, **119**, **120**
drawers, 8, **8**, 42-43, **43**, **75**, 114-122
  drawer-guide hardware installation, 117-120, **118**, **119**, **120**
  fronts, drawer front installation, 121-122, **121**, **122**
  hardware, drawer-guides, 117-120, **118**, **119**, **120**
  kitchen pantry drawers, heavy-duty construction, 93, **94**
  materials used in drawers, 114
  organizer, 98-99, **98**, **99**, **100**
  routing rabbets and other grooves, 114
  side-to-bottom assembly, 115-116, **116**
  sizes, 114
drill presses, 38-39, **38**, **39**, 67
  plug cutter attachment, 68, **68**
drills and drilling, 19-20, **19**, **20**
  bits, 19, **19**
  clutch feature, 20
  countersinking screws, 19, **19**, 67, **68**

shelving, 5-8, **5**, **6**, **7**, 63-64
  basement shelves, 49-50, **50**, **51**
  brackets for wall-supported units,
    29-30, 30, 61, **61**, 63-64, **64**
  Lazy Susan revolving
    racks/shelves, 95-97, **96**
  metal support tracks, 39-41, **39**,
    40, **41**, 63-64, **64**
  pegboard-sided shelving, 35-37,
    35, **36**, **37**, **38**
  Plano unit, 5, **5**, 6
  plywood shelving
    improved, 32-34, **32**, **33**, **34**
    simple, 31-32, **31**, **32**
  portable ladder shelf unit, **7**, 8
  prefabricated shelving units, 31,
    31
  pull-out shelving unit, **75**
  toy and book storage shelving,
    77, **78**, **79**
  wall-stud supported shelving, **6**,
    8
  window, above-window shelving,
    61, **61**
Simpson Strong-Tie Connector Co.
  Inc., 135
sink installation, 107, 125-128,
  126, **127**
skylights for light and ventilation,
  10, **10**
sources of materials and tools,
  131-136
spackling compound for walls, 27,
  28
spade bits, 19, **19**, 67, **68**
Speed Square, 13-14, **14**
squares, 13, **14**, 65-67, **66**, **67**
Sta-Put Color Pegs, 135
stains, 27, **28**
stairways
  attic stairway unit install, 53-56,
    53, **54**, **55**, **56**

under-stairway storage, 71-73,
    71, **72**, **73**, **74**, **75**, **76**
  under-stairway work center, **76**
Stanley Works, The, 135
  closet organizers, 83-87, **83, 84,
    85, 86, 87, 88**
stiles, cupboards and cabinets,
  111-113, **112**, **113**, **114**
Structron Corporation, 135
stud finders, 24, **25**, 30, **30**
suspended-ceiling storage space
  in garage, 47-48, **48**

T
table saws, 17, **17**
table, pull-out table, **75**
tape measures, 13, **14**, 65-67, **66**,
  67
tool support/holders, 61, **61**
tools, 13-24
  accessories, 14-15, **15**, 22-24
    air compressors, 14-15, **15**
    clamps, 22-23, **22**
    nail-holder, 14, **15**
    nailing guns, 14
    orbital sanders, 24, **24**
    planes, hand and power, 23-
      24, **23**, 36, **37**, 111, **111**
    sanders, 24, **24**
    sanding blocks, 24
    stud finders, 24, **25**, 30, **30**
    stud finders, 30, **30**
  acquiring necessary tools, 13
  air compressors, 14-15, **15**
  angle drill, 19, **19**
  bits, drill bits, 19, **19**
  blade positioning when sawing,
    18, **18**
  brooms, brushes, dustpans, 28
  chop or compound saw, 16, **16**
  chuck, drill, finder/driver
    chuck, 20, **20**